DON'T PRESS SEND

A MINDFUL APPROACH TO SOCIAL MEDIA
AN EDUCATION IN CYBER CIVICS

KATIE DUFFY SCHUMACHER

ISBN-13: 978-0692731819
ISBN-10: 0692731814

TO MY PARENTS, MARY AND ED DUFFY,

who, through their kindness toward others and their generosity of spirit,
taught me the importance of being community-minded.

TO MY HUSBAND, JEFF,

who took the time to open his heart to this project, enabling me
to explore this venture and pursue my passion of empowering children.

TO MY THREE CHILDREN, MICHAEL, BRIAN, AND JILLIAN,

I thank you for forging through with me as I spread the Don't Press Send
Campaign's lessons in cyber civics to your peers and community.
This is no easy task for a teenager, and I love you all the more
for soldiering on with me!

IN LOVING MEMORY OF MY FAITHFUL FRIEND, SUNSHINE

For sitting loyally and patiently by my desk as I wrote, rewrote
and edited this book, hoping for your walk to come.
I miss you more than words can express.

ACKNOWLEDGMENTS

I am blessed to have so many people to thank for helping make this book and this program become a reality.

To Kevin Anderson & Associates for guiding me through the writing, editing, and publishing process with true professionalism.

To my new friend Kira Breed-Wrisley, who heard my voice and helped make my dream come true.

To my lifelong friend Pam Ryan Jahn, whose simple question "If not now, when?" gave me the push I needed to begin to write.

To Dr. Jolie Silva from New York Behavioral Health, who changed my life by introducing my family and me to the practice of mindfulness. Her wisdom and knowledge has helped me to guide many students and their parents.

To George Stamboulidis and Kim Maynard from BakerHostetler for their sound legal advice that secured and protected my work and my logo.

To Scott Richman, who has been with me on this venture since the very start. His technical knowledge has put the Don't Press Send Campaign on the social networking map, his vision has given us a website, and his patience has given me sanity.

To my niece Caitlin Schumacher, who took my logo design and made it a reality, and introduced me to the world of Facebook and social media. Cutting and pasting a video was a two-day lesson. I have come a long way, thanks to you.

To J. T. Kirby, for his beautiful cover design.

To the Rockville Centre School District and community, which supported the Don't Press Send Campaign program and provided me a platform on which to begin to educate about the importance of cyber civics. A special thanks to South Side Middle School Principal Shelagh McGinn, who endorsed this idea from the very start; Assistant Principal Rose Cammarata, whose excitement to educate was contagious; and Assistant Superintendent Dr. Noreen Leahy, who continued to encourage both school and community to partake in this venture.

To the Rockville Centre Don't Press Send Parent Committee, whose support gave me the courage to expand my program and create parent workshops. A special thanks to Anna Casavecchia, Pam Jahn, Jill Livingstone, Lara McCarthy, Penny Stamboulidis, Nancy Travers, and Meri Woythaler.

To the many other parents, some of whom some I never even met, who took the time to spread the word about my program and its importance. Much appreciation goes to Principal Libby Trencheny of Lakeside Elementary in Merrick, New York, for being the first school outside of Rockville Centre to believe in my program.

To the many student volunteers who helped spread the word by posting on their social media sites, hanging flyers, passing out bumper magnets and wearing T-shirts. A special shout out to Kelly Jahn, our senior staff writer from South Side High School, and to the many other students of South Side Middle and High Schools for the many hours of putting together packets for presentations. I thank you all.

To my family and friends who took the time to read my manuscript before it went to print and gave me their honest opinion: Diane Condon, Patty DelBello, Eileen Doyle, Pam Jahn, Dr. Noreen Leahy, Shelagh McGinn, Mary O'Leary, Claire Rotondo, Jolie Silva, and Penny Stamboulidis.

To the many schools and organizations that have invited me to present the Don't Press Send Campaign's workshop to their students and parents. I thank you for being members of a community that cares.

Hats off to the more than 15,000 students who took the Don't Press Send Campaign's Pledge. I thank you for forging the path in creating a cyber community that will be a place of mindful behavior, kindness, and respect toward one another.

Ill. TABLE OF CONTENTS

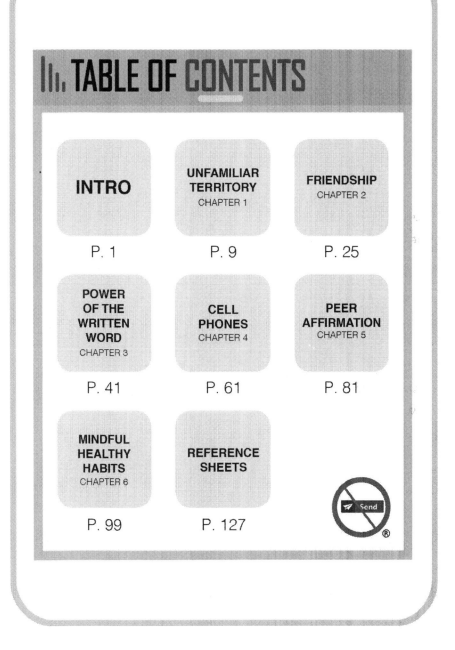

INTRODUCTION

» What is mindfulness?

Mindfulness is paying attention on purpose, learning to live in the present moment, and being actively engaged in the here and now.

» What is cyber civics?

Civics models the behavior for responsible citizenship. **Cyber civics** teaches the same lessons as they pertain to online behavior.

HOW MANY PARENTS have gone back to a school, a gym, a friend's house, a field, a park, a beach, or a pool with our children in search of their phones? I have seen the panic on the faces of my children and their peers when they have misplaced their phones. Many of my children's friends have come to my front door to search my house frantically from top to bottom as if it were a police raid, flipping cushions on the couch, moving furniture, and asking everyone in the family (including the dog) if they have seen their phone. The search is usually followed by the statement, "My parents are going to kill me if I lost my phone!"

It is clear that we have taught our children one hard and fast rule about cell phones, **don't lose it**.

When I ask children and teens what guidelines their parents have given them when they got a cell phone for the first time, they say, "Don't lose it; don't break it." Children take this to heart. My friend's daughter used a phone with a cracked screen for a year, one on which she could barely read her messages. I was impressed that her parents were teaching her to be more careful and responsible with her things, and that they had made it clear they were not going to spend money on a new phone before it came time for her upgrade. As parents, we have thought a great deal about teaching our children responsibility for the devices we give them. We have ingrained in them, "Don't lose or break this, it's expensive." But was this nearly enough? Now we need to direct our attention to teaching them, "Use this safely, kindly, carefully, and with good intent."

When we give a child a cell phone, in addition to saying **if you lose this you're in serious trouble**, we need to say **if you use this in an unkind manner, there are serious consequences**.

It is an unfortunate reality that the onset of technological exposure for today's children is getting younger and younger, which in itself worries me in terms of their social, emotional, and brain development. For myself and my teenaged children, the "relationship" with technology began somewhere around seven or eight years of age, with handhelds, from LeapFrog to Game Boy to PS2s to computers, tablets, iTouches, and eventually having their own cell phones at the start of middle school. As a parent and educator, I now realize I gave my children few guidelines or rules to prepare them for what was coming ahead. Would I allow them to drive a car without providing clear rules and guidelines to ensure their safety and the safety of others on the roads? Would I not warn them about texting, speeding, listening to loud music, or otherwise driving distracted? About drinking and driving? Would

I not clearly explain the consequences should they not abide by the rules? Of course I would. I would warn them that breaking those rules could result in serious injury or death to themselves or others. Would I allow them to swim in the ocean without making sure they knew how to swim and were aware of the dangers the ocean could pose? Would I fail to caution them never to swim alone, and to be aware of their surroundings? Of course I would warn them that ignoring these guidelines could result in drowning and death. It is obvious that we need to do a better job of discussing the pitfalls of technology with the same concern as we do with any other topic that could have a negative or dangerous outcome, such as drinking and driving. As parents, we cannot control what our children choose to do or say, but for me, I get some comfort in knowing that at least I have told them or warned them. There is no stopping free will, but I hope we can be that little voice in their heads that hopefully will help them stop and think before they act. I know for myself, even as a grown woman I hear my father's booming voice, and my mother's kind compassion for others, helping to guide my choices.

I think we as parents need to realize that we have given our children devices they are often not mature enough to handle. Many years ago when we purchased a computer for our home, we placed it in the kitchen because we were concerned about the possibility that the children might use the Internet in ways that were unsafe or unwise. I know I did. That way, I could monitor what my children were doing while they explored in a public, supervised space. At that time I knew better than to give my children their own computers in their rooms at such a young age. Yet smartphones are exactly that—hand-held computers our children carry with them all the time. We failed to realize that in giving our children cell phones, we were giving them access to a world they are not emotionally mature enough to handle.

Even writing this, it amazes me that we missed the boat. It seems so obvious in retrospect. Perhaps it was because of the speed with which cell phones changed: my first cell phone was not a computer. In my case, I initially gave my children regular phones, but when a smartphone was the next free upgrade, I did not think twice about the potential problems they could cause or what I was giving them access to. I did not realize or consider that moving to a smartphone was such a big jump, and I did not anticipate how my children would adapt to the easy Internet access of smartphones or what the implications of that would be. I did not foresee the problems they could encounter. They adapted to a very unhealthy attachment and way of communicating, as well as having the freedom to access any piece of information, and have unlimited access to age-inappropriate sites. I try to shield my children from the worst sensationalism on the news, but with a smartphone, they have access to much, much worse.

As they say—when you know better, you do better. Providing our children with guidelines and strategies to foster kind, healthy interactions while using technology is extremely important. One possible strategy is to give a child a cell phone with limited access, perhaps giving them a phone for emergency calls but holding off on getting a data plan until the child is older, and restricting Internet use to a common area in the house. Although we did not do this on purpose, many of us did fail to fully consider the consequences of giving our children these devices.

This is why I began the Don't Press Send Campaign: to better educate and empower students to use technology kindly and safely, by providing them with structure and guidelines to easily follow.

The Don't Press Send Campaign began in September 2013 in my hometown of Rockville Centre, New York, with the support of our local schools, both private and public, and the backing from parents. The Don't Press Send Campaign visited each school, addressing students from third grade to high school, spreading our message of using technology with good intent. Word began to spread outside of our little community, and the Don't Press Send Campaign began to take off. It is evident that parents and students are hungry for this program. To date, I have given numerous presentations. It is my belief that most children do not set out to harm, but because of the emotional disconnect the screen creates, our children may not be aware of the impact they might have on others, and they may have assimilated an emotionally detached approach to digital communication. Within these presentations, many students have shared their experiences, both good and bad, and have educated the Don't Press Send Campaign as much as we have educated them.

Throughout this book you will hear firsthand how our children are growing up with social media as a central part of their lives. We need to look at two important factors:

1. How we, as parents, can better equip them to use technology
2. How we can find a healthy balance and teach them to use mindfulness as they pause before they post.

These factors will help to create a kind cyber community by strengthening their empathetic skills.

Having presented the Don't Press Send Campaign guidelines and strategies to many schools, I realized it is simply another conversation we need to begin to facilitate in our homes and schools. There is nothing in this book or in my presentations that requires a teaching degree. As parents, we are our children's first teachers. As an educator, I was taught that creating clear rules and guidelines helps to foster a secure, stable environment in which children can better learn both educationally and emotionally. Children feel safe, secure, and less anxious when they know what the rules are.

In one of my graduate school classes, a teacher described the importance of structure and guidelines clearly. She had us break into groups and gave us an assignment. One group had clear rules and guidelines. The other simply had a topic. She said it was to be handed in the next class and was worth 40% of our grade, then dismissed the class. As you might imagine, the group given only the topic were very anxious. Many, if not all, of the students had called her, leaving messages with questions about the assignment on her office phone before the next class, asking for details. I was among the many students bewildered by the lack of direction in the assignment. We, of course, did not have cell phones, so we did not even have the relief of immediate feedback, which only served to add to our anxiety.

The following day when we walked in the room, the anxiety was palpable among the topic-only group. The teacher came in and explained that this assignment was a clear example of what you as a teacher will create if you do not provide clear rules and guidelines for your students. She explained that they do not need to be detailed, but they do need to be clear and understood by all. Children feel safe and secure with clear rules and guidelines and, believe it or not, they want to adhere to them.

I believe that our children have unfairly been given few or no rules or guidelines pertaining to the use of technology. After presenting at many schools, it is clear to me that many of today's children need our help and assistance in creating guidelines. It is my hope that we, as parents and educators, can begin to provide our children with the ability to use kind and careful communication: "cyber civics." Many children may think this is not needed, but I can assure you, they need our guidance as they learn to navigate the technology we have chosen to give them.

On the adjacent page, you will find the Don't Press Send Pledge. This is the backbone of the Don't Press Send Campaign. The Pledge was developed after speaking to many students of all ages and hearing firsthand how technology and social media are so difficult for them to navigate. After visiting a variety of schools, I have revised the Pledge many times and believe it has become a good, solid foundation for children to draw upon. In reinforcing the Pledge, parents and educators can begin to better prepare our children by giving clear, direct guidelines for them, as well as a springboard for some much-needed conversation both at school and at home.

After reading each chapter, you will clearly see how the Don't Press Send Pledge was established and why we, as parents and educators, need to encourage and enforce these guidelines. Having our children strive to adhere to this Pledge will help create a kinder and safer cyber community for all. It is my hope that together we can help strengthen our children's empathetic skills and encourage a mindful approach to social media. Enforcing these cyber civics skills will enable us to stomp out the epidemic misuse of technology.

DON'T PRESS SEND PLEDGE™

» I will carefully choose who I allow to have my cell phone number.

» I will not give anyone account information such as passwords or answers to security questions.

» I will choose followers/friends with the understanding that not everyone is my "true" friend.

» I will not type or send messages that I would not say face-to-face.

» I am aware that "the screen" creates an emotional disconnect, and I will choose to use Kind and Careful communication.

» When reading any text or post, I will remember to mindfully respond and not impulsively react.

» I am aware of the dangers that anonymous sites and apps present and will choose not to partake.

» I will ask permission before taking and/or posting photos or recordings of anyone, valuing my privacy and respecting the privacy of others.

» I will not send any pictures or videos of myself or anyone else without clothing on.

» If something is making me feel uncomfortable or unhappy, I will make the choice to unfriend, unfollow, delete, block, turn off, or step away from my device.

» I will keep open communication with a trusted adult regarding online interactions.

» I will not post group pictures of an event, knowing that exclusion is very hurtful.

» I am aware of the dangerous habit of posting things in order to get a number of "Likes."

» I will not have my cell phone accessible during homework hours and will set a reasonable time for it to be docked for the evening.

» I will choose to use an alarm clock, and not a cell phone because I know it creates an unhealthy attachment and will prevent me from engaging in potentially harmful dialogue.

» I am aware of the ramifications of my actions if I send something that is inappropriate or hurtful to another and how it could affect my future.

» I promise not to send any pictures or texts that do not show respect to others or myself.

» I will try my best to use Kind and Careful communication while using all technology and share my knowledge with my peers to aid in the "DON'T PRESS SEND" Campaign.

CHAPTER ONE
Unfamiliar Territory

» What is a community?

A **community** is a place where people live, learn, work, and socialize in a particular place. A cyber community is a place where people work, learn, and socialize online.

RAISING CHILDREN WHO have grown up with technology has put many of us in a difficult position. Many parents feel that their children are more capable of understanding and utilizing technology and social media than they are themselves. For some parents it is extremely intimidating; even turning on the TV and programming the DVR can seem like a daunting task. As children, we socialized in our communities, on our streets, and face to face. We are equipped to teach our children those guidelines and rules, but unfortunately, they no longer apply in today's society. Like it or not, our children are living primarily in a cyber community, and they desperately need some guidance, rules, and strategies.

Many children are glued to screens, whether televisions, phones, computers, gaming systems, or tablets. Maybe they are pursuing adventures in learning, connecting with kids on the other side of the globe, or doing research for school with access to resources we could only have found in the Library of Congress. For many—if not most—children, these screens are their primary mode of communication. Some have their own phones as young as third grade or maybe even younger. We did not grow up with this technology; most of us adopted it only as adults, and even then, we are not familiar with the programs our children are using most frequently. This leaves parents at a disadvantage; it can feel like being illiterate while trying to guide our children through the reading process.

Because we did not grow up with this technology, it is easy to be intimidated by it, or to turn a blind eye to what our children are engaged in. Because we do not understand what they are using it for, many of us have simply left the technology to the children. But leaving them alone with the technology means leaving them without guidance, and without boundaries. We have all heard horror stories of kids who have had compromising photos sent endlessly around the Internet to their peers, and subsequently of kids being bullied for months on end by their classmates. In the worst cases, we have heard of children who take their own lives because it seems like the only way to escape humiliating, ceaseless, and/or violent online abuse. Whether we know it or not, we have probably all known children who have been harmed in this way to some extent. So how can we help our children to be safe in an environment we do not fully understand, or perhaps are phobic of ourselves?

We have the perplexing opportunity of raising our children in a time period very different from the one we grew up in. Like parents on the cusp of the Industrial Revolution, we are raising children in an unfamiliar world, the "Technological Revolution." We are trying to help them navigate problems we ourselves have never faced. The task feels challenging—technology changes so quickly that keeping up with every new iteration of online communication is impractical and trying feels like a losing battle. As soon as we understand one form of online communication, the kids have moved on to three more.

The first step is admitting we have a problem. This is, for many of us, a problem we thought we should never have had. Many parents of this generation are better educated than our own parents, and many of us thought we would be equal to the task of keeping up with our children's education. We are equipped to teach so many things—after all, knowledge is power. We just failed to realize the "power" would come from an actual outlet!

However, just because we are not familiar with the technology does not mean we have to abandon it like the lawless Wild West. Cyberspace can feel too big to police—it is too unregulated to make rules and enforce them, and too convoluted to track and monitor users, even when those users are our children. Because legislation cannot keep up with the fast pace of technological change, creating an app or site in which kids partake is extremely profitable. It seems like little thought goes into the damage that can be caused, especially on anonymous sites. As it takes time to create laws that would protect and shut these sites or apps down, they can cash out at the expense of our children's psyches. But that does not mean we have no power to help our children use technology with good intent. We can teach our children how to protect themselves from becoming victimized and, just as important, from victimizing others. No one wants to see their children hounded by peers, and no one wants to think their child is capable of this level of cruelty toward others, but with the barrier of the screen, children may unintentionally be unkind without even realizing what they are doing.

Just because we are not logged on to the latest programs does not mean we cannot teach our children how to behave on them and help them find a proper place for technology in their lives. As we know, technology is not a fad. A good place to start is by creating a healthy, open dialogue with your children or students about the opportunities and pitfalls of technology. We can encourage them to take advantage of the opportunities, like exploring their interests in-depth online, while also helping them avoid the pitfalls, like unhealthy attachment to their devices.

As parents, our primary purpose is to guide our children and educate them so that they can apply what they've learned as they go through life, whether face-to-face or through technology. We have to guide them to say **if I wouldn't say this to someone face-to-face I shouldn't type it** because the rule is the same online or off, **be kind**. They will learn for themselves how to use the technology, but we will be the ones who teach them how to interact with others, teaching that the values of kindness, empathy, respect, and mindfulness apply in all aspects of life. We teach our children to stand up for one another, to be kind, to treat others as they want to be treated. Just as we teach them to be cautious and look both ways before they cross the street, we also need to teach them to be cautious online. We should be teaching our children to apply these same rules and values within their "cyber community."

The intimidation of technology itself may be the reason we hesitate to set boundaries and guidelines. If we put our fears aside together we can provide our children with some "cyber civics"—careful, kind communication. Parents and educators need to provide a foundation for their children and students as they try to navigate the sometimes overwhelming technological world in which they are growing up.

Preventing Harm and Teaching Kindness
» What is empathy?

Empathy is the ability to emotionally relate to and share the feelings of others.

MANY CHILDREN DO not knowingly set out to hurt others via the Internet. The problem with communication through the filter of the screen is that we cannot see the other person's reaction to the things we say. Nonverbal cues teach us just as much as the words we say aloud. A tilt of the head, a facial expression: these things tell us something before the words come out of the other person's mouth. Before children understand language, they understand facial expressions. If we are hearing a language we do not understand, we can tell whether the speaker is angry or happy. A comment on a web page can be made quickly, and the writer can navigate away and forget about it, not pausing to consider that the person on the other side of the screen will see those words and take them to heart. Anyone who has perused an Internet comments section—on a blog, a news page, or even on a social network where people ostensibly know one another—has seen how quickly commentary can devolve into vicious sniping. This is not a problem limited to young people. Most of us tend to be less thoughtful when we are not speaking face-to-face. This, I believe, is where the dialogue begins. We can take out a cell phone and say to our children, "See this screen? This is what separates you. This is what disconnects you from the people you are engaging with." We need to teach our children to look past the screen and remember that there is a person, with real feelings, on the other side.

Part of this is inherent in the screen itself. When we speak in person, we can see the harm we do; human beings are social creatures, and from a young age we are finely attuned to the emotions and reactions of others. Most of us will back off when we see we have hurt someone, even someone we do not like. But when we cannot see that reaction, we lose the impetus to stop and think. Without the immediate feedback of a hurt response, children and teens may push too far, perhaps not realizing the harm they are doing.

Compounding this is the public aspect of the Internet. An exchange or argument among a few friends can be harmful enough when it goes on in private, but once it is public, the entire school can watch, and worse, join in. One student pressing the "like" button may seem insignificant, but when multiple students press "like" all at once it becomes a bombardment that seems impossible to escape. As an adult this would be difficult to confront; I cannot even imagine it for a teen trying to find their way. The detachment of the screen can be exacerbated by the anonymity of the crowd. With many people commenting at once, each individual can feel less responsibility than if they were commenting alone. After all, if fifty people are saying the same thing, how much impact does one more have? But the result is that what might once have been a private disagreement can turn into a mob attack.

Worse still, the permanence of written communication can drive home attacks in a way that shouted insults never could. Because it is written and tangible, a child can read negative messages over and over again. Instead of fading as the memory diminishes, the message can become stronger with time. Because kids are in constant contact with mobile devices, there is no way to escape hurtful communication. Once upon a time, home would have been safe from vicious classmates, but now messages can continue after school and into the night. Students who are targeted can feel like they have no respite, and the situation can spiral out of control.

Because of this detachment between users, technology can work against empathy, which means that as parents we need take extra care to teach and model *for* empathy. We need to talk honestly about how easy it is to detach when we are separated by the anonymity of a screen. Children need to learn to pause and be mindful before they post, and think, **If I were to receive this, how would it make me feel?** Teaching our children to respond rather than react is a simple yet powerful lesson when using social media.

Educating for Mindfulness

THE DIFFERENCE BETWEEN a reaction and a response is in that mindful pause. Reaction is immediate—something happens, we act on that stimulus without thinking. That is a reaction. For instance, a child receives a text message making fun of a classmate. Instantly, without thinking, they react with a reply. A response comes after a moment's thought. The stimulus occurs, and instead of acting with impulse on it immediately, we stop and make a conscious decision about what we will do next. We can teach our children to stop and be mindful, to ask themselves, **How would this make me feel?** The action they take next is thoughtful, not automatic. This is not a reaction, but a response. The term "cyber community" is one we sometimes see used casually, referring to a group or forum on the web, but it is worth thinking about what a real cyber community might look like. We can ask ourselves— and our children—what makes a community? How can we support one another online as well as offline? Who do we want in our community, and how do we want to treat one another? We need to remember that while the methods of communication we use online are different, the people behind the screens are the same.

Many young students report having 100, 500, or even thousands of friends on social networks. We need to help our kids interpret what it means to be a friend. If your network is 1,000 people wide, how many of those people can truly be a part of your community? When friendship is a numbers game, it is easy to forget that you are essentially among strangers. Another way to think about friends online is to couch it in terms of access: the question is not "Do I want this person to be my friend?" but "Do I want to grant this person access to my private life?"

Educating about Laws and Rules

WE HAVE ALL done stupid things as kids. We have all gotten caught up in the moment and made choices that we would probably be mortified to have brought up in front of others, or things we try not to think about ourselves. Maybe we once spread a nasty rumor about someone, maybe we exposed ourselves emotionally and were humiliated, or maybe we just wore an outfit in appalling taste. Now imagine that outfit, that rumor, that declaration of teenage love, searchable by anyone with an Internet connection, forever.

This is the world our kids are living in, where their choices, good and bad, follow them around from place to place, all the way into adulthood. I know that I have made many mistakes in my life that have long since been forgotten by me and hopefully by anyone else. This is called "growing up." Unfortunately for our children, this is not their reality, which I think is unfair. It is giving them a distorted view of themselves (poor self-image) and interfering with their emotional growth. We should learn from our mistakes, move on, and hopefully grow as a result. Today's kids do not have that luxury.

When children insult one another on the playground, the adult response is often to let it go—it's just part of growing up. We may have been told "you won't remember it in ten years" when we had a disagreement with another student. But because everything on the Internet is permanent, the things our kids do now *will* matter in ten years and could affect scholastic and job opportunities.

Recent anti-bullying legislation like New York State's Dignity for All Students Act enforces consequences for students who attack others in cyberspace, meaning that instances of acts considered cyberbullying can go on a student's permanent record. This can include everything from leading a direct attack on another student to simply clicking "like" on a post made by someone else. Few students set out to bully others, but what may feel like just a joke that got out of hand to the perpetrator may be officially considered cyberbullying, which is now being taken more and more seriously by schools and by the community at large.

Under the Dignity for All Students Act, these incidents can be documented in the student's permanent record at the school's discretion, meaning that depending on the severity, it may follow them through their college application process. In some instances, the consequences of perpetrating a cyberbullying offense can even follow a young adult into the working world as they seek employment. Given increasing awareness of how serious the consequences of Internet harassment can be, teens with documented involvement in cyberbullying incidents are making themselves less viable candidates for college admissions and for future jobs.

A student I was told about recently was a star athlete; he was a high school football all-star, and he, his parents, his coaches, his teachers, and his friends all believed he was sure to be recruited to a college team. Indeed, a prestigious university came to see him and was on track to select him for a scholarship—but did not. When the student asked why he had been passed over, he was told that the recruiters had read through his Twitter feed and decided that his tweets were not representative of what the school was about. To the student athlete, his tweets were presumably just for fun, but the school could not take the risk of admitting him. In a world where Internet photo sharing and communication is easier than passing notes in class, kids sometimes seem to immortalize every moment of their lives to share with friends. But because those photos are forever, every ill-conceived decision that makes it onto someone's photo page will be there in the future for anyone to see, whether it's a future employer looking at pictures of underage drinking or a future in-law accidentally finding a topless selfie.

For many young people this may seem as if I am catastrophizing. That time seems far in the future, and the probability of getting caught seems remote. So many corners of the Internet feel private—they are talking to "friends" on a site they are familiar with. It is easy to forget that even "private" profiles are often searchable to strangers, or to friends of friends. While most kids have a particular audience in mind when posting to the Internet, such as their school friends, many more people will see it. We need to remind our children that **not only is everything online permanent, nearly everything is public as well**.

Finding a Healthy Place for Technology

TECHNOLOGY IS NOT the problem. All-or-nothing approaches to technology are impractical—can we really prevent kids from using their phones? But more than that, casting technology as the enemy does not make any sense. Using computers, kids can access information in seconds or communicate with family and friends all around the world. Having a cell phone on hand means kids are less likely to find themselves stranded with a broken-down car or at a party where everyone around them has been drinking and they need a safe ride home. GPS means they are less likely to get lost. On numerous websites, teens can meet others struggling with common difficulties, learn about political issues, and share writing and artwork. Technology opens all kinds of doors for our children, and they should be encouraged to learn and explore. Technology is a tool, and our task is to teach our children how to use it, not to vilify it.

Young people should feel empowered by technology and use it with good intent. It is our responsibility as parents to help them make better, safer, and kinder choices. Helping our children build a healthy relationship with technology is what is needed.

Part of setting guidelines for technology use has to do with teaching kindness, mindfulness, respect, and empathy, and part of it is taking time to really detach from our screens when we do not need them. This might mean a "phone curfew," where all of the family phones are turned off after a certain time in the evening or left in another room while kids are doing home-work. It might mean docking phones outside the bedroom at night, so that the temptation to check messages every ten minutes is easier to resist. Most online harassment among teenagers happens between 9:00 p.m. and the early hours of the morning—just staying away from the phone at those times can mean your kid avoids those interactions altogether. Turning off the screens at the same time each evening gives an opportunity to reset, to unplug, and to think about technology's place in our world.

When we use technology in the manner in which we do, we are actually sending a message to our brains, telling us, "Don't remember that, your phone has got it covered." The process of creating memories is short-circuited and redirected because a device is doing what our brain would ordinarily do. For example, when you take pictures of an event, your brain gets the message, "You don't need to remember that, it is in your phone's memory." It is being saved somewhere, but it is not being saved in your mind as an emotional memory—it is being stored in a device. This fact about brain development was very eye-opening to me because using and recalling information is vital to our brain health.

The human mind adapts to new technologies, letting go of things we used to store in our own minds. Many of us who grew up before the cell phone era remembered dozens of phone numbers—those of our friends, our family, the local movie theater, or a pizza place. In fact, to this day, I remember the old phone numbers of all of my childhood friends, but I do not know the current number of anyone outside of my immediate family. I don't need to—my phone has it stored in my contact information.

This has happened before: many of us forgot how to do all but the simplest math when we left school, knowing we could rely on a calculator. To reach back even further, the rise of literacy brought about one of the most dramatic changes in memory that humanity has ever seen—before we could depend on the written word, oral histories, folk stories and songs, and even epic poems like *The Odyssey* were stored in the minds of the creators and the tellers. Once we learned to write, we no longer needed that talent, and so we lost it, to give space to other things.

Obviously, I am not suggesting that we return to a preliterate society. The ability to pass off mental tasks to devices and processes that can perform them more efficiently and conveniently is often a good thing. However, I do believe that we must examine what we are giving over to our technology and consider whether this task, this process, is worth losing, and ask ourselves: are we giving up too much for convenience's sake?

The loss that worries me is memory. Our memories are, fundamentally, who we are. Our experiences shape us, and our memories become the stories of our lives. But how do we store them? I do take photographs, and always have. My friend Pam can remember which outfit I wore on our fifth-grade field trip, but I was not blessed with that kind of memory, and so I do want that external record. When I think back to my wedding, I think of my photo album; when I look at the photographs, they take me back, and I remember more details about that day. The photographs are not the memory, but they help me to remember. There are very few pictures of me as a child; I was the youngest of nine and as you can imagine there was very little time for photography. There are of course pictures of family parties, like communions, weddings, or graduations, but none of me alone. Some of my siblings have actually tried to pawn off pictures of my older siblings and claim they were of me. As I got older, I got wiser, and I realized that the math did not add up: my brother could not have been five while I was a baby—he is thirteen years older than me! Therefore, capturing my children's childhood in pictures is important to me. Having records of their development and the events in their life is something we look back at and cherish. However, the taking of photographs should not be allowed to dominate events to the point that they **become** the event.

I see young people documenting every moment of their lives, and it seems to me like they are missing out—the point of a photo is now the photo op and not the savored memory. Because they can see the pictures immediately, delete the unflattering ones, and take them again, the photograph is the focus of the shot, not the moment, the event, or the place. Not long ago, when we took photos on vacation, there was a kind of mystique to it. You would come home, take them to the developer, wait to have them returned, and finally see them again, as a kind of way to relive the trip. You waited to see what the Colosseum looked like and if your hair was a mess while you stood next to it: that is how you looked that day. You wanted to see if the Northern Lights had shown up in a picture as beautifully as they did in person, if a photo could truly reflect the majesty of what you had seen. You did not have the option of taking photo after photo until you got one where you looked perfect, and I believe that when we do that, we are editing not only our scrapbooks but our very memories. We are moving through life, not as a whole movie, but an orchestrated frame-by-frame edit.

When my kids were in fifth grade, most of their friends had received their phones as graduation gifts. The school had an end-of-year dance, and I was one of the parents working the party. Very quickly, the dance devolved into huddles of children taking pictures of one another, and nothing else. No one was dancing, no one was talking, no one was even standing awkwardly against the wall in the tradition of middle school dances—the event had become a giant photo op.

Recently my friend's daughter graduated from college and went to Europe with some friends. They had been planning the trip for almost an entire year, and when she returned I excitedly asked her about the trip. Instead of spilling out stories and chattering away excitedly, she simply handed me her phone, and said, "Swipe left, there's a lot of them." Indeed, she had hundreds of photos, and she appeared to be having a good time in them, but it struck me as I scrolled through them that the pictures were themselves the outlet for her excitement. It was as though by taking the pictures, she had exhausted her need to talk about the experience, and yet, by spending all her time taking them, she was not fully immersed in what she was doing, and now back home, she was not fully immersed in sharing about what she had done. I also know that many of the photos I see young people taking so avidly are never seen again. They are stored in their phones and computers, maybe a few are posted to Instagram or Facebook, but all that documentation does no good if it is never visited again.

I do not need my children to see the world, or to remember it, exactly the way that I do. The world changes, and we all must adapt. But I am concerned when it seems that the way in which they use technology is getting involved in their working memory, impeding their ability to form the kinds of memories I have learned over the years to treasure. I want them to be able to live for the moment and not be overly concerned about how they look, but rather to be focused on the experience itself. One of my favorite quotes—often attributed to Abraham Lincoln—is, "It's not the years in your life, it's the life in your years." We should be teaching the importance of living and creating memories, not the importance of documentation.

Teaching Mindfulness

EDUCATING KIDS ON how to interact with technology can seem like it raises a lot of negatives: don't take that picture, don't write that message, don't send that email. But there is a chance here to focus on the positive—on what it means to set aside technology from time to time and to thoughtfully, mindfully, live in the present moment.

We teach our children in many ways, but modeling behavior is what sends the strongest message. We have all been to restaurants and watched entire families go through meals with each individual glued to their own separate screen. Recently, my friend Pam sent me a photo of a sign outside her favorite breakfast shop that said, "We Don't Have WiFi: Talk to Each Other." It is obvious that many others agree with the Don't Press Send Campaign's message about finding technology's place: not here and not now. I would love to see more restaurants adopt a "no cell phones at the table" policy. We can certainly insist on this policy at our own dinner tables. Many of us have spent time with—or even been—that person constantly interrupting an in-person conversation to check messages. Mindfulness for our children begins with mindfulness for ourselves. The more accessible we are, the more constantly busy we can be. But are we busy out of necessity, or are we just busy being busy?

We have all known that person whose vacation photos are so extensive that we wonder if they managed to do anything besides take photos. It is worth thinking about whether, in the rush to commemorate an event, we are missing the whole thing while taking pictures to post online and send to friends. Are our kids doing the same? When we go to a party, someone has put in the time and thought to host it, to invite us, to welcome us to their event: we are there to celebrate with them, to talk to our friends, to dance, to enjoy where we are and who we are with. If everything becomes a photo opportunity, a chance to post pictures of ourselves having fun, when do we actually have that fun?

Many of us who have spent time with screens, for work or for fun, have found time slipping away—what we thought was a five-minute email check turns into two hours of surfing before we realize what is happening. Just as screens create a distance from the people we are communicating with, they can take us out of the world around us and lure us into hours of mindless clicking. Stepping away from the screen not only gives us a chance to reflect on what we are posting and how we are affecting others, it gives us the opportunity to look around and take stock of how we are living.

Just as communicating through screens can create an artificial detachment from the people we are interacting with, the nature of instant communication can override even the strongest impulse control. When posting a picture or a message is as simple as clicking a button, or when checking how many "likes" you have is as easy as constantly refreshing a page, the repetitive task can be addictive. Particularly for teens already prone to impulsivity, it is easy to get locked into a feedback loop of post and refresh, and even easier to post thoughtlessly. Taking a step back and pausing before posting is difficult, and it must be a conscious decision. We need to help our kids break that cycle.

Mindfulness is about respect, both for ourselves and for those around us. It is being conscientious and aware of what we are doing and what is around us. Teaching our kids to be thoughtful about their cyber communications is part and parcel of teaching them to be thoughtful about how they live their lives.

The Don't Press Send Campaign encourages kids to pause and think—to be mindful—about what they are about to do. We can encourage our kids to pause and take a breath before they post a picture or send a message, and ask:

» **Is this something that would feel good if I received it? (Empathy)**
» **Could this be misinterpreted? (Perception)**
» **Am I reacting or responding? (Mindfulness)**

Sometimes it will be fine to send—there is nothing wrong with using the Internet to communicate. But we all need to learn to slow down, to think, and to consider how the person on the other side of that screen will feel.

While many of our children's grandparents think, *"When are these computer gadgets going to be over?"* they are here to stay, so finding technology's place for our children and ourselves is imperative. As we know, with any kind of change, we need to tread lightly and not give our children the sense that technology is bad—because it is not.

I love that I can order groceries online and get places using my GPS. My children love that they don't have to go to the library and get the *World Book Encyclopedia* out to find information, and that they can communicate with relatives who are not close by.

It is my hope that together as parents and in our communities we can better equip our children to find a balance and not have technology completely consume their lives. I, for one, would be heartbroken if our children go through life missing many of the similar good and bad experiences that we have had ourselves. If they are looking down at screens too often, it will alter and limit their emotional interactions with others. Life will pass them right by, and opportunities will be missed. This is not something I would wish for any child.

CHAPTER TWO
Friendship

» What is a friend?

A **friend** is someone who is trustworthy, loyal, and kind.

SOMEWHERE ALONG THE way, our children have learned that "more is better" when it comes to accepting friend requests. We have seen, time and time again, our children's personal feelings, thoughts, and photographs being passed around to others, who really are not true friends. This has caused our children to open their worlds to large numbers of acquaintances—and possibly strangers—who have no regard for their privacy. From the start, we need to replace the idea that "more is better" with "less is more," and teach our children to keep their circles small.

In my experience, students of all ages, from third grade through twelfth grade say the same things when I ask them to describe a friend: a friend is trustworthy, loyal, kind, and respectful. A friend is someone who has your back. Some say they share similar interests. But how can we teach our children to recognize who has those qualities?

Even offline, or as I call it, real life, as an adult, it takes some thought to decide who our true friends are. It can be a long process, where we see them in many contexts, at their best and perhaps at their worst. Making good friends takes time and insight. Online, it is far more difficult: when our children develop friendships over social media, they have far less information about the person they are getting to know, often not even that person's real name. Even when a child is interacting with peers he or she knows from school or extra-curricular activities, the emphasis on having large numbers of online connections means that many of the "friends" a child has are kids he or she would not even invite to their home or want to hang out with. When talking to our children about their use of social media, we need to teach them that a friend means the same thing off or online. When a child receives a friend request, they can begin to become comfortable with only accepting friend requests by *their* criteria of what a friend is.

How many friends can one child have? Through middle and high school, many children and teenagers report having hundreds or even thousands of "friends" on social media sites; the number gets higher the older the child gets. But how many of those people can be considered actual friends? The maximum number of connections (not just friends) a human being can maintain is 150, including family, friends, classmates, teachers, neighbors, coaches, doctors, tutors, parents of friends, and casual acquaintances: everyone you know. One hundred fifty might sound like a large number, but it includes everyone you interact with semiregularly; the number that can actually be considered friends is only a small fraction of that. No matter how popular you are, there is an upper limit; if you add more connections, some of the old ones will suffer and fall by the wayside. This means that by definition, most of a child's 1,000 social network friends are not their friends at all.

Years ago, when we were children, there was some thought as to whom we befriended and when and where we saw them. Our friends had to call us on the shared house phone and talk to other family members to get through to us; when we played together we rang each other's doorbells and met our friends' parents in person. Although children do and will partake in things their parents know nothing about, our parents most often knew with whom we were spending our time.

Today, more and more friendships take place in a cyber community. Moving into the online world is a little like moving from a small town where everyone knows one another to a large city where you are surrounded by strangers. In the small town, there is not only face-to-face contact, there is reputation. In a large city, people need to be warier; there is less security if you do not know the majority of people you interact with. The problem with a "cyber community" is that at the moment, in many ways, it is not yet a community. I consider a community a place where there are rules and laws and where neighbors look out for one another and respect one another. Clearly the Internet itself cannot be made transparent, and there are no official rules or laws in place for their cyber communities. However, any community should be a place where respect and boundaries are always considered. Just as we want our children to feel safe and secure in our communities, by providing guidelines and boundaries, we can help them create a kinder, more respectful cyber community in which to spend their time.

Who Gets Access?

FRIENDSHIP, REAL FRIENDSHIP, is a gift. We need to teach our children to ask themselves, what is it that they are giving and getting when they make a new friend? There are many subtle nuances governing what friends give one another within a relationship, what kind of friendship exists between two people, and how much those two people will share. Most of us have miscalculated a friendship at one time or another and told a secret we later regretted sharing. Online friendship can present risks. Just from looking at their social media pages, our children can see exactly what they are granting their "friends" access to, and it is important that we help them scrutinize those decisions.

Our children allow their friends to see different things based on what they share on social media sites, what others say about them, who their friends are, and, of course, what pictures they post. As long as the posts are thoughtful and the friend group carefully selected, this should not be an unmanageable problem. However, when our children "friend" as many people as possible but post information as though it is going only to true friends, that is where they can run into trouble. We need to help them stop and think when adding friends, **Do I want you to have access to everything I have ever shared online? Do I consider you a trustworthy person?**

We can help our children think about their online friends in other contexts and ask, **Would I grant this person access to these things in any other setting? Would I invite this person into my home?** Most children do not like everyone they go to school with, nor should they. Although they should be taught to respect their peers, one of the difficult lessons of growing up is that you will not like everyone, and (more ego-damaging!) not everyone will like you. However, when it comes to online "friends," our children are willing to grant access to friends and even strangers they would not want to share a cafeteria table with. We can help them to consider online friendship by two criteria: either they can choose only to "friend" people who are in fact their friends offline, or they can accept and live by the tenant that online friends or followers are not the same thing as real friends and proceed accordingly. In other words, know your audience.

Just as important as asking our children to whom they are granting access is asking what they are being granted access to. Another issue with the friendships children develop online is that they are working off of limited information. Not only have they never met many of the people they are interacting with, but the persona everyone chooses to present on the Internet is usually carefully portrayed. We have all heard stories—or even had firsthand experiences—of predators who seek out children online and entice them into inappropriate relationships with lies and coercive tactics. But even nonpredators are rarely being completely honest about who they are by what they portray.

It is important to talk to our children about the fact that a social media profile is a distorted reality. We can ask them what they post and why. Will a child post a photograph that makes her look glamorous and happy or one that shows her with messy hair or a bad outfit or with spinach in her teeth? Will he mention the scholarship he just won, or the test he just flunked? This is not to say that we should not encourage them to manage their online presence—indeed as social media become ever more ubiquitous and searchable, it is imperative that they do so. But all of us, even parents, need to bear in mind that the Internet story is never the whole story; it is only one side of the story—the good, pretty, and perhaps more glamorous side.

If a child sees his or her best friend's flawless profile, he or she should be able to remember that same friend getting whiny and grouchy when he or she gets hungry, or missing the winning goal in a soccer game. For people we really know, the reality of who they are goes beyond that social media veil. But for the people our children meet only through the Internet, that idealized portrait is literally the only information they have to go on. Not only is it not enough information, there is no way of learning more and no guarantee that any of it is even true. Unfortunately, our children have learned to compare their lives to the story of the flawless portrayal that others choose to share. For example, our children might look at a classmate's wall and see them Jet Skiing in Mexico, yet their family may be in financial crisis. As adults, hopefully we know we can't judge a book by its cover; however, I have seen parents fall prey to becoming overly interested in adult peers' walls or posts, causing them to judge themselves and imagine that someone else's life is better. I was recently on a lovely skiing vacation with a friend who was constantly checking Instagram and looking at the pictures of other families' vacations to see who was where. After a while, it began to feel as though she was more invested in comparing her vacation to other people's vacations than in actually experiencing her own.

Children have always, and will always try to fit in. It may be hard for us, as adults, to recall what it is like to be a young person trying to find their own identity, always questioning, *Am I normal?* Or, *Am I popular?* I hear children saying, over and over, "I won't do that, that's weird, it's not normal, it's not popular." I remember the same feelings as a child, believing that there was a baseline for "normal," or "popular," and constantly watching what I did, what I said, and what I wore, to make sure I was in line with that baseline. Children since the dawn of time have relied too deeply on the opinions of peers, over-valuing normality and popularity in a way that takes precedence over their own personal needs and desires. Fortunately, for us as children, normality, or lack thereof, was not on public display.

It is as though every child has their own billboard, which they are constantly comparing to everyone else's billboard. Growing up this way cannot be easy, and all this comparison works against building one's own self-confidence. Taking good care of our children's emotional well-being may sometimes mean steering them away from this online arena of comparison.

At one of my presentations, a boy told me a story that was heartbreaking, but his mother's actions were something to admire and learn from. His father had recently passed away, and his mother told him that he would not be allowed to use any social media for a year. She did not want him faced with seeing other children's happy family photos, references to their own fathers, or even kind condolences, until he had had some time to heal from such a great loss. After he shared his story I said, "You have a smart mom, and I think she gave you some great advice." I explained that I, too, had lost my father, and I know how hard it is, hoping he felt my sincere empathy. I said to the room, "Your mother did absolutely the right thing. The loss of your father is a personal struggle, and you will be stronger, and heal better, if you are not faced with social media." Even things meant kindly can hurt when someone is in the middle of recovering from such a trauma or loss. If someone posts a picture or happy memory of his father, this could interfere with his grieving process, which I am sure would never be anyone's intent, but it needs to be considered. People who are not his closest friends and family are not part of this personal process and need to respect the boundaries to allow for healing to happen.

Personally, I consider it risky to post a picture or a comment about some-one who has passed away who you are not intimately close to. Taking the chance that your comment or picture could be taken in a harmful way or hit a nerve that should not be exposed at any given time is a chance of causing pain to someone who is healing. Grieving is personal, and some people prefer to do it in private. On the other hand, some others may choose to be more public and share it on social media. But it is their healing process, and that must be respected. Those boundaries should be honored. If it is not your immediate loss, maybe you should not post, even if it was a happy memory. We must remember it is not up to us to decide what is public and what is private: it is up to the person who is grieving to decide how they want to heal.

A few years ago, my friend lost her father. As anyone would be, she was deeply distressed at this terrible loss. Throughout the year, she makes mention of him on her Facebook wall. On Fathers' Day she writes a tribute to him: "Happy Father's Day to Dad in Heaven!" On his birthday, "Happy birthday to the best dad on Heaven and earth!" When she posts pictures of family events and parties, she writes things like "We are missing Grandpa today," or "So glad my angel, Grandpa Joe, is looking down on us." Incorporating her father into the record of her life is a part of her healing process.

I always respond to these posts. When I first saw her doing this I was surprised. I did not understand why someone would make her pain, her loss, so public, inviting others into something I would have kept far away from the spotlight. I realized, however, that this was her way of healing, of keeping her father present in her life even when he could no longer be there in person, and so as her friend I always write something nice. "You are so lucky your children have an angel watching over them," I write. Or, "I know he must be so proud of you." Though I do not fully understand what she is doing, I want her to know she has my support, and I want to help her continue to move forward through her grief.

This is a place where the "like" button can be used to good effect. Many people, when faced with another's grief, find themselves tongue tied, uncertain what to say. Nothing can make it better, and that can lead us to think that anything we say will only make it worse. Adults and children alike can find themselves at a loss when encountering someone else's pain, leaving those who are grieving feeling isolated in their sorrow. "Liking" a post such as my friend's, or leaving a brief, supportive comment, small gesture though it is, can let her know that she is not alone.

On the other hand, I have seen hurt come from the other direction, though I know it was never the intent of the people posting. I was told about the tragic and unexpected death of a teenager on the cusp of his high school graduation, which, of course, shocked and devastated his family, his friends, and his entire community. His twin sister managed to bear up through her grief and move on with her life, though she would never forget him. Ten years later, when she was planning to return for her class reunion, her brother's friends began posting pictures of him on Facebook. "So sad that Jimmy will miss it," people wrote. "Won't be the same without Jimmy." Or, "I know Jimmy will be looking down on us from Heaven."

Jimmy's sister was taken aback to see these things appear on her social media feeds. Though she had moved on with her life, he was still her brother, and when she took moments to think about and honor him, it was on her own terms, in a place and time where she felt safe, and able to cope with the emotions that cropped up. Regardless of how well-meaning those sentiments were or how real the sadness of her classmates, seeing those pictures appear out of nowhere left her grief-stricken and brought her unexpectedly back to the worst moments of her life. This caused her to question whether she could handle going to the reunion at all. Once again, it was well-intended, but that was not the effect.

Reopening a wound that is starting to heal is never our place. We must understand that what we post and what we say in online public forums has an impact on those who see it. Maybe if it is not your immediate loss, like that of a parent or spouse, you should not express your feelings or thoughts about it. Again, most people do not do this intending to cause harm, but can set someone back who is trying to move forward.

Friends of Friends

ONE OF THE particular pitfalls of social media is the "friends of friends" phenomenon. For one thing, it can create a false sense of endorsement—a motivated person can work through a friend group, with everyone believing they are a known quantity, when in reality they do not know anyone at all. It is easy to assume someone is safe if they are a friend of a friend, but when our children allow friends of friends into their networks, they are no longer relying on their own judgment but on the judgment of their friends. The vetting process is now one step further removed. Practically speaking, on some sites it is even possible for "friends of friends" to see information on your page that you might have thought of as private, such as something your friend posted to your page and everything associated with that post. (For this reason it is a good idea for kids and parents to take some time to see what the profile looks like to the public and to friends of friends, to make sure they know what they are sharing, and what is visible to whom.) Essentially this means that a child is not only giving access to the people he or she knows, but to second-degree contacts that he or she has never met. Even if a child trusts her friends completely, can she trust all of *their* friends? Impossible.

Even if a child does trust their friend to be a good friend, they also need to be able to trust that friend to make good decisions about their personal information. Much as secrets tend not to stay with the original confidante, screen names, phone numbers, and passwords can be passed along from one person to another. Being thoughtful about who our children give their cell phone numbers to means guiding them to ask not only, **Should this person have access to me via cell phone?** but also, **Do I trust this person not to share my cell number without asking permission?** Children need to be taught that their cell phone number is private information. I, for one, do not appreciate when I get a call from someone I have not given my number to personally. I am careful about who I give my number to, and getting a call from someone I have not shared it with and being told, "Oh, your friend gave me your number," feels like a violation of my boundaries and my privacy. I don't like this happening to me, and I certainly do not want it happening to my children.

The barrier of the screen in social media communication affects not only *with whom* our children interact but *how* they interact. The detachment from in-person interactions can lead children to be more thoughtless with their communications and to forget exactly who might be seeing the information they post. Creating a "cyber community" means guiding our children to become good "cyber citizens" and to think about how they can be good friends to others online—once again, reinforcing the concept of keeping our circles small.

Everything Is Public

WHEN WE TALK to our children about *who* has access to them, we also need to talk about *what* they have access to. Because social media contacts are called "friends" on some sites, and because most children's networks do in fact include their actual friends, it is easy to forget that everything they put online passes out of their control. Whether because of a mistake in privacy settings or an unscrupulous "friend," anything and everything posted online has the potential to be spread around the school, the city, or the world. Private emails and texts may seem safer because they are going to smaller, handpicked groups, but even then, a child's privacy is only as secure as the people he or she has put trust in. Anyone can take a screen shot and share it with whomever they want. Today most phones are capable of taking screenshots of what is sent to them, including written text as well as photographs. Our children need to be aware that nothing is private in regard to technology. Once it is out there, there is no getting it back.

Eighth-grade student Petra shared her story of a false sense of friendship with me. She confided in a very close friend that another girl was making fun of her, and Petra shared how that made her feel. Because it was a private text, offline, to someone she trusted, Petra thought what she was sharing was in confidence. Although she asked her friend not to tell, her friend then screen-shot the conversation and sent it to the girl she was talking about. I share many things with my close friends, and that should be a safe thing to do. But putting these things in writing can come back to haunt our children when someone they trust turns out not to be trustworthy.

This is, of course, not a phenomenon that arose with technology. Most of us can remember rumors spreading when we were young, secrets being shared without permission, or even notes where students wrote down terrible things about classmates and passed them around the class. What is new is the degree to which secrets, pictures, and quotes can be disseminated and the large number of people they can reach, as well as the great speed with which this can happen. As if that were not bad enough, having harassing messages on the screen and easily available means that the recipient can read it over and over, reinforcing the negative message 24/7.

One of the most common and cruel examples is that of the child who sends nude or otherwise inappropriate photographs to someone he or she trusts, only to have them sent all around the school. Children have been tormented, dropped out of school, and even become suicidal over this violation. While the people at fault in these scenarios are the people passing around the photos and harassing the subject, the reality is that the child who posed for the photos lost all control of what happens to them as soon as those photos left their possession. I am happy that there are laws in place to protect our children against child pornography, but our children are unaware that even the photos they take and share among themselves may be considered child pornography.

This seems to be a growing problem that many communities are dealing with. I have been made aware of numerous instances in many schools with children as young as sixth grade choosing to send a photo without clothing on, either of themselves or someone else.

We do not want or need to teach our children that no one should be trusted—that is a terrible lesson and one they should not have to learn. But circumstances change, friendships end, and we are dealing with children who are all trying to find their place and fit in. We need our children to learn to treat all online communication as something that leaves their control once they share it. As they say, never put something in writing if you wouldn't want to see it on the front page of the *New York Times*. As a child, I used to hear, "Would you kiss your grandmother with that mouth?" This is something that taught me to be accountable for what I say. I learned that in my home and my community there was a proper way to speak and act, but when I was with my friends I knew I could get away with cursing and acting in ways I couldn't in front of my parents. Our children do not have that luxury—what they say, write, and take pictures of is all documented. Though many things are just kids being kids, because it is in writing it looks worse, and there are greater consequences.

False Sense of Friendship

DECIDING WHO ONE'S friends are can be a difficult proposition. Having someone ask to be your friend is flattering, and not accepting a "friend" request on social media can feel like an unnecessary rejection—if someone wants to be friends, it feels rude to say no to them. Simply the fact that we call online connections "friends" or "followers" can shape the way we think about them. And mundane online communication can create a positive feedback loop: a child posts something, their contacts "like" their posts, and they reply. It can feel like those "friends" are closer than they actually are, and clicking "like" on a comment about a pop star is an act that has virtually no content, but the approving communication reinforces the idea that this person is an actual friend.

An online community can also create a sense of belonging. We are social creatures—everyone wants to fit in, teenagers more than anyone. Being part of something, being liked and valued and respected, feels vitally important. Being a part of social media groups means that our children can feel like part of the "in group," and having hundreds or thousands of friends can make them feel popular, or make them appear popular, even if those hundreds of friends are people they do not even know.

Just because the nature of friendship online can be misleading, that does not mean it is always bad. It is not our duty to teach our children that online communication is the enemy. Technology is a tool, and our mission should be to guide our children to make positive, safe choices and to proceed with caution by acting with good intent. For many young people who feel isolated in their communities, who have interests that none of their classmates share, or who are fascinated by a topic or cause, communicating online with other children and teens can be a revelatory experience and can allow them to expand their horizons in ways that would have been much more difficult for our generation. Children may join communities dedicated to art, politics, or social issues. They may find relief from their own difficulties by talking to others in the same situations, and some may indeed make what feel like real and lasting friendships. Our job is not to stop them from taking those steps, but to give them the tools to make wise choices while exploring.

Talking online in a group devoted to their favorite artist is not in itself dangerous; it only becomes dangerous when children forget that the people they are talking to are not actually people they know.

I recently learned of a fifteen-year-old girl who met a nineteen-year-old boy on an anonymous blog. He talked to her about their shared interests and issues and quoted lyrics from songs she loved. However, his interest in her soon turned dark. He hacked into her account, installed malware, and found personal information about her and her family. He asked her to fly to meet him, and when she refused, he threatened to kill her family, providing details that proved he knew where to find them. He knew her parents' and siblings' names and their work addresses. Terrified that he might carry out the threat, the girl got on the plane and flew to meet the forty-eight-year-old man who had posed as her friend. She was not tracked down until a week later, a week that she spent alone with a predator, being sexually abused and tormented. Most of us have heard other stories like this one, of young people who are coerced, threatened, or bribed into meeting predatory adults who abuse them. While most children will not end up in such dire circumstances, it does happen to some, and we need our children to know what to do to protect themselves. No matter what, our children need to know they can come to us. It is imperative that we teach our children that even if someone is threatening them, they can and should share that with us and we will help them. There is always help available.

Although this person got info by hacking, our children also need to know that unscrupulous people can skillfully get information from them without their realizing it. Answering seemingly innocent questions can add up to giving someone enough information to track you down in person. Just as identity thieves can get far by knowing your mother's maiden name, your pet's name, or other answers to banking security questions, people seeking to harm a child can track them down with their name, where they go to school, what after-school activities they participate in, and other things that might seem to flow naturally in conversation. We need to teach our children to recognize what should be private and then help them to stand firm on not giving out their personal information—again, asking, **Should this person have access to this information?** They need to feel confident and capable of stepping away from an interaction or a group if someone is being inappropriate or making them feel bad or uncomfortable. Our job is to help them protect themselves and lead them into good judgment.

Of course it is not as simple as teaching our children to restrict their online communication to true friends. Even in tested, personal relationships, loyalty and trust can be hard to come by. Many of us have had the experience of someone we thought was a close friend turning out to be not so loyal or trustworthy. The friend who turns on their closest friends is a staple of high school movies and has been for years, and even the most well-meaning of friends can err unintentionally and do damage to someone they truly care about. We need to help our children learn to choose their friends carefully but also to act as though everything they post could become public—because it very easily could.

Mindful Friending

THE SOCIAL LANDSCAPE online is difficult to navigate, precisely because children do not always know with whom they are dealing. While hard and fast rules can be helpful, they will not cover every circumstance perfectly. Should a child "friend" their friend's cousin? Their neighbor who moved away three years ago? Their piano teacher's daughter? Their lab partner's older brother? Because it can be hard to know where the lines should be, it is important that children learn to take a breath and take note of what is really going on in a situation. This is not always so easy to do.

Instinct is not always perfect, but we can help our children learn to assess interactions online, especially if something "doesn't feel right," and the signs are the same as they would be in a face-to-face interaction. A child can stop and ask themselves:

> » **Is this person being too pushy, or trying to get me to say or do something I don't want to do?**

» **Is this person acting like we are closer than we are, or asking me questions inappropriate to our relationship?**
» **Is this person putting me down, or flattering me too much?**
» **Is this interaction making me uncomfortable, or unhappy?**
» **Is this making me feel unsafe or fearful?**

Whether it is a stranger trying to get too close or a classmate trying to manipulate a child into saying something embarrassing, we need to let our children know that it is always okay to stand up and walk away from the screen. After all, that is one of the best things about online communication—you do not need an excuse; you can just turn off the computer and end the interaction.

Online communication can be a positive thing, but we need to help our children think carefully about what information they are putting out into the world and with whom they are choosing to share it. Whether a friend request or an online chat, it is always good for a child to be mindful, and ask:

» **Have I met this person face to face?**
» **Would I invite this person into my home?**
» **Does any part of this interaction make me uncomfortable or unsafe?**

As parents it can be scary to watch our children forge ahead into a social world we have no connection to, where we cannot be familiar with all of our children's friends. We cannot necessarily stop them from connecting with people we do not know, but we can help them to be mindful of their safety and guide them to take precautions for their own privacy.

CHAPTER THREE
Power of the Written Word

» What is mindful online communication?

Mindful online communication is pausing before you post and carefully considering who will see it and how it may be perceived.

THE POWER OF the written word has several facets: there is what is said, how it is said, and how it is perceived. How I intend something to be heard may not be the way it is understood and vice versa. Because of this, it is important that our children learn to communicate in ways that are less easily misunderstood. They need to consider the mood and mindset of the person hearing it. They also need to realize it is not just what they say, but also how they say it. There really is no way of knowing what is going on in someone else's life or where they are coming from on a particular day or what subjects or jokes may hit a sensitive nerve. Each and every one of us will hear something differently depending on how we are feeling, and we need to guide our children to stop and think, not only about what they intend to say, but about how it may be received. We need to teach our children that if they are not sure how their message will come across, they should talk in person or try to rewrite the message. In the business world, people do not keep typing back and forth when something is misunderstood; they speak to one another. Even in this technological world, people still take meetings. Lots of them. If someone is clearly not understanding me, I pick up the phone or speak to them in person and make sure I am understood. In writing it can be difficult to convey nuance, tone, or mood, and if the subject matter is delicate or likely to be misinterpreted, it is a good idea to rethink putting it in writing at all.

During my visits to schools, many students have shared their experiences of unkind words being used without any regard for their feelings. On a recent visit to a middle school, two girls came up to talk with me after my presentation. They told me that when I talked about the power of the written word, it reminded them of something that happened to them. Some of the boys in their class had put together a social media site where they "rated" girls in their class, placing them on either the "ugly list" or the "pretty list."

As I listened to these two equally adorable seventh-grade girls explain what transpired, they explained that one of the girls talking to me had been placed on the "ugly list." She said that she had always been insecure about her looks, as most thirteen-year-old girls are, but that her parents and friends had always reassured her that she was more than attractive, and she took comfort in that. The "ugly list" had confirmed all of her worst fears about her appearance: that everyone thought she was ugly, and worse, that others (these boys) had thought about it, laughed about it, and posted her "ugly" status for the whole school to see. Her confidence was shattered.

Her friend had been hurt by the lists too, but in a less expected way. The boys had placed her name on the "pretty list." This dubious compliment, rather than making her feel good about herself, made her feel self-conscious and judged, even though she had been judged "pretty." Worse, her friends got mad at her—they saw her name on the "pretty list" and began snubbing her and telling her "You think you're so hot." She was treated as though she had participated in the making of the list, as though she were stuck-up and as though she were the cause of the hurt feelings of the girls who had been placed on the "ugly list," even though she had nothing to do with the making of the site. No one benefitted from this. Perhaps these boys were unaware that this list would cause such pain. They are not girls and do not look at themselves the same way, and they may not have been aware of the pain and humiliation that their written words had caused. We need to teach our children not to rate each other, but we also need to teach them to consider the perspectives and feelings of the people they are talking about online.

Written Words Are Permanent

NO ONE GOES through life without getting their feelings hurt. That is just part of life. Learning to let the negative opinions of others go and not take them personally is all part of the natural maturation process. As parents, we may tell our children to ignore a slight from a classmate. But when we talk about the kinds of things sent through social media, it is not as easy for them to let go as it was for us. The written word carries much more power than verbal expressions because of its permanency, and because of the ability to reread messages over and over, twenty-four hours a day, seven days a week.

Written text is inherently different from a verbal comment. If a child says something mean to another in the hallway, it might sting, but it is often over as soon as the moment has passed. Though the comment may hurt, it is easier for a child to learn to put it out of his or her mind and move on. But when children are texting and messaging one another online, the comment or insult is there to stay on the child's phone or computer. Children are also aware that the comment may have been sent out to many of their peers via others' contact lists, meaning that in addition to dealing with an attack, they have the anxiety and humiliation of knowing that it is likely public. Children can revisit messages over and over, reading them again and again at any time of day or night. The more they read it over, the more they think about it, and that reinforcement makes them internalize it. Repetition makes what should have been trivial take on an unhealthy place of importance.

When we were young, meanness at school could be terrible, but at least when we went home at the end of the day, we had respite. At home, if we were lucky enough, we were safe—even phone calls were unlikely to be private enough, or frequent enough, for serious harassment to occur. But now, when our children want to communicate, they can be in constant contact, and this means that if a child is being harassed, there may truly be no escape. Added to this, most of our children's online communications are entirely private from us. Rather than a shared family phone, where parents would at least be aware of constant calls, children communicate on their private devices, so that we may not know if they are spending minutes or hours a day communicating with their peers, or if they are receiving several messages a day or hundreds, or if the words are kind or unkind.

Anonymous Sites Are Dangerous

UNFORTUNATELY, ANONYMOUS SITES are available to our children, and they pose a problem for several reasons. Anonymity is in itself dangerous—when our children do not know to whom they are talking, they can open themselves to threats emotionally or even put themselves in physical danger.

Recently I learned of the murder of a thirteen-year-old girl who had been communicating with an eighteen-year-old stranger on the anonymous app Kik. He gained her trust and convinced her to meet him in person, and when she did, he murdered her. This is a horrific act. Dangerous encounters occur on the devices our children are using, but they are preventable if we better educate our children. We need to be aware of the apps and sites our children are on and to strongly enforce that anonymous sites are off-limits.

Any site or app in which someone can hide their identity is unsafe. When people can write things anonymously, it creates an arena where no rules apply and it becomes any easy place to prey on the vulnerability of children. Some-one who claims to be fifteen years old might really be forty-five. Someone can pretend to like all the things you like to grab your attention and seduce with their keyboard. On anonymous sites, pedophiles or otherwise dangerous individuals can easily gain access to a victim.

One example of an anonymous texting application is called Yik Yak, an application that lets users create "yaks," text messages that are sent to everyone within a ten-mile radius who has the app, without identifying the sender. In schools where this app has been adopted among the students, it causes chaos. This is a story I heard about the damage that can be done via anonymous sites. A student named Rebecca walked into the park and saw a large group of her schoolmates staring at their phones and laughing. Because all students had downloaded Yik Yak, an anonymous mass-texting site, everyone received the same text about her at the same time: "Rebecca couldn't get a date for prom," said one. The next said: "Guess she couldn't find a forklift to pick her up!" At first, Rebecca didn't understand what was happening, but she too had the Yik Yak app, and so she got to see what was being said about her directly. She knew everyone was seeing it and laughing at it, but she had no idea who was sending the messages. As one would imagine, this was devastating to her, as it would be to anyone, to know that all your peers had received a degrading message about you, while you were standing right there vulnerably, where they could all see your reaction. Many of us have had the feeling that we are being laughed at, at one point in time or another. When anonymous texting apps like Yik Yak are used, children have absolute proof that the laughter is real and no proof of where it came from.

Anonymity on these sites is also one-sided. Though the perpetrators of the jokes at Rebecca's expense could have been anyone, she herself was clearly identified. She could not pretend to herself that they might be talking about another Rebecca, and she had no way of knowing who was saying what. Anyone who has been the subject of a vague rumor knows what it is like to look around at a classroom or group of friends and think, *"Who is saying these things about me? Are my friends really my friends at all, or is it all a persona?"* Our children will encounter conflicts and disagreements, but we need to teach them to confront those honestly and to stand behind what they say, not to obscure their opinions behind the safety of an anonymous site.

Yik Yak has also caused more serious disturbances in schools. Shortly after it appeared, one school in Chicago was overrun by teenagers texting vile messages to and about one another, until the administration was forced to close the school for the day because of the mass hysteria the app caused. In other places, it has been used to call in bomb threats and threats of school shootings. Though so far these seem to have been pranks, the anonymity of the app has allowed people to threaten the lives of others without fear of consequences or accountability. We need to teach our children that if they participate in anonymous sites and messaging, there is a big chance that one of two things may happen: they will get hurt, or they will hurt someone else. Even children who believe that, by only reading and not posting, they are doing no harm, need to understand that just by being an audience to cruelty, they are still participating in it. When it comes to anonymous sites, it is best not to partake.

Having presented at many schools I have come to realize that each school, district, or organization has its own cell phone and technology policy. Some schools give their students iPads as an educational tool. Some allow students to use their own personal phones as an educational tool, to retrieve information via the Internet—if a question comes up in class, students may simply look up the answer. I feel that allowing students to have personal phones during a school day presents an overwhelming challenge for schools and teachers to deal with. iPads provided by the school are hard enough to manage, and they are monitored by the district. I can only imagine how hard it is for a teacher to ensure that all of the students in a class are only using their personal cell phones for educational purposes.

Even if children are texting with their own phones, texting during math class is still texting during math class, and it is still a distraction. Unfortunately, many parents push for their children to have their cell phone accessible during the school day. Parents can always call the school's office and have important information relayed through them. In most schools, the administration would almost certainly prefer having their staff mildly inconvenienced to having students constantly distracted by their phones.

It is each parent's personal decision whether or not it should be our job to monitor all the communications our children have—they are growing, learning to engage with their social world, and we must each decide for our own family how much privacy we are willing to give them to navigate this new territory. Regardless of where we decide to set our limits, as parents, we do need to talk with our children about the ways in which they are using technology to communicate and help guide them to avoid the endless loop of obsessing over messages and chats that are actively hurting them—even those that may not have been intended that way, especially on anonymous sites.

It is not only that the physical written word makes comments harder to escape. The reality is that most of these communications are not just happening one-to-one in a private chat. The communication happens openly on social media, and they are visible to a whole audience, which, in most cases, includes a large number of their peers, some of whom may decide to join in and some who simply read the comments. An unkind comment made privately is bad enough, but children who are being harassed online are also being publicly humiliated. The nature of social networks makes it easy to publicly attack, and for everyone within the "friend" circle of the children involved, to pile on to the original comments. We may want to tell our children to forget about it when they are being harassed, but when online circles bring it to such a level, our children may not be afforded the luxury we had to simply put it aside. Everyone may not press the "like" button or post a comment, but a child knows that most of his or her peers have read what is being said about him or her.

When I was a child, my parents would tell me to let these things go, to let insults roll off my back, to toughen up. Having eight siblings certainly helped me to build that thicker skin early on. If I were insulted or got into an argument with a peer, my parents might ask what I said in response or imply that I was being too sensitive. They were not wrong to say this—learning to handle these things is a necessary part of growing up. Resilience is a crucial skill that children must develop, and I am thankful, looking back, that my parents allowed me to fall and expected me to pick myself back up, so that I learned that skill. They taught me to realize who my real friends are, to learn to grow a tougher skin, and to build a stronger sense of self. This has helped me throughout my life and it has aided in my teaching. Technology may require our children to build yet another layer of resilience.

We should not be too quick to dismiss online harassment as simple childish sniping. For children being harassed over the Internet, the insults can be relentless and vicious and can feel like they are coming from everyone they know. Additionally, encouraging them to stand up for themselves and say something in response can just prolong and exacerbate an online war. Most adults could not stand up to that kind of a trial with equanimity, and we should not expect our children to do so alone.

I am finally beginning to see some backlash and recognition by parents of how important it is to take a strong stance against cruel and abusive online comments. Former Red Sox pitcher and World Series champion Curt Schilling recently spoke out about the comments made online about his daughter when he posted a tweet congratulating her for being accepted to college, where she would soon be pitching softball. After a few congratulatory replies, he began to see something terrible: strangers were posting vulgar, sexual, and grotesque things about his daughter, things that shocked even a man who had spent most of his life in locker rooms.

Schilling responded by posting the names and tweets of the people involved. One tweeter lost a college scholarship and another lost his job with the New York Yankees. When a White House correspondent tweeted something unpleasant about one of the Obama children, President Obama fired her the next day. This makes me wonder, what were these people thinking? Did they truly believe that they would not lose their jobs over such inappropriate tweets? Our children have grown so accustomed to writing and posting their every thought and feeling that they do not think twice about it, even when they reach adulthood. As parents we need to remind them that their online actions have real-world consequences. We also need to recognize the intensity of public online commentary, and, like Mr. Schilling and President Obama, stand up for our children when they are targeted.

Emotional Barrier of the Screen

WHEN I WAS growing up, mean things were sometimes said to me, and I sometimes said mean things to others, but I learned quickly the consequences of saying something hurtful to another child, because I could see their reaction right in front of me. I could see the hurt look on the other person's face, and I physically felt the guilt and discomfort that came with knowing I had hurt another person. These natural consequences that we experienced taught us many things regarding interpersonal communication and relationships. Much thought would go into looking someone in the eye and insulting them, not only because they might just lash out, or perhaps deliver a punch, but because saying something mean in person means physically seeing the emotional impact of those words and feeling the discomfort within yourself.

Online, the screen causes an emotional disconnect. When children cannot see the person on the other side of the screen, it is harder to imagine that the words they are typing have a direct effect on someone else. It is easy to type and send without thinking, or write things that we would not say face-to-face, because there is no immediate consequence for doing so. Not seeing the hurt means it is easier to imagine it is not happening. This emotional disconnect concerns me very much, both as a parent and as an educator. If we allow our children to become more and more disconnected emotionally, what kind of adult relationships will they have? What kind of fulfillment can you truly have if you do not allow yourself to be emotionally present?

If it is easy for an individual child to minimize the impact of their actions online, it is even easier to abnegate responsibility as part of a crowd. When a child sees a comment about a peer and thinks up a clever retort, it takes seconds to type and post it, and there is no risk or confrontation involved. The rapid pace of Internet commentary works against the need to stop and think before speaking. Replying is quick and easy, and even more automatic is the "like" button, where a child can show support for a statement without a second thought. The word "like" is very powerful in itself. Young people strive to fit in, to be accepted, and "liking" something is an instant way for them to show that they are part of the group. Receiving a "like" is tangible confirmation that they have succeeded, that they are approved of, that they are liked. By turning a blind eye and accepting that the "like" is just part of this generation, are we allowing our children to learn that peer approval plays a greater role than internal strength?

When multiple children rush to comment and "like," each child can feel less and less like their own comment matters—after all, who is going to notice one comment among a hundred or more? Because the Internet is public, commenting on social media can be a kind of performance, each child trying to show that they fit in or to one-up others by saying something funnier or more unkind, forgetting that at the center of all this is a single child, who has been made a target. That child will not just notice one comment among a hundred or more; that child will notice *every* comment, and will see how many dozens of peers and even friends are jumping in to attack, by the number of "likes." To the perpetrators it may feel like a harmless game—after all, each of them only said that one thing, or just "liked" someone else's comment—but to the targeted child, it is devastating.

As parents, we do need to teach our children resilience—we need to help them to grow strong, so that a mean comment will not destroy their sense of self. But we also need to recognize that online, petty meanness can quickly spiral into crushing attacks that should not be minimized. We need to teach our children that, just like their vote counts even in a nationwide election, their comment or "like" counts, even if it is only one among hundreds. Even if everyone else is saying the same thing, our children need to pause, take a breath, and ask themselves, **How would I feel if someone said this about me?** This will reinforce their empathetic skills. If they would not say it face-to-face, there is no reason to say it in writing.

Perception and Intent

I KNOW AS an adult I have had trouble perceiving intent with online communication. We do not realize how much we rely on body language until we try to communicate without it. Most of us have received emails or online comments that were unsettlingly ambiguous—did "nice sweater" mean "I like that sweater" or "you look ridiculous"? Did that smiley face indicate happiness or sarcasm? Short, to-the-point emails can come across as brusque and dismissive and genuine compliments can sound facetious. Even with good intent, we can hurt one another online. If this is so difficult for adults, how much harder must it be for children, who are still learning the nuances of social interaction?

Teenagers are still learning how to navigate their social hierarchies, so they are highly attuned to anything and everything that is said to or about them. Depending on their mood, a child might put the best or the worst possible interpretation on an online comment. In some ways, the ambiguity of tone online can be even more anxiety-producing than if someone was directly unkind, leading the recipient to go over and over it in his or her head, wondering what the other person meant.

Norah and Grace found themselves dealing with written ambiguity when Norah missed a school field trip they had been excited about. Grace emailed Norah:

"Hope you got something nice at the mall! Lucky you, missing the trip cause you were 'sick.' LOL j/k love you."

When Norah read the email she had no idea what it meant: Did Grace think she had lied about being sick? Was she joking about thinking Norah was lying? Had someone told Grace that Norah was lying? Norah had no idea how to respond, or even what was going on. Grace may have simply been kidding and expressing regret that they had missed the trip together, or she may have been rudely accusing Norah of ditching her. Whatever her intent, the result was that Norah was left anxious and unsure of how to respond.

Interpreting tone is hard enough for adults; it is even harder for children. This means that when writing online, children need to learn to read over what they have written and imagine how it might sound to the person receiving it. The way something sounds in our heads is not always the way it sounds to someone reading without context or tone of voice. **Teaching our children to proofread for intent can be a useful skill**.

One way that the online world has dealt with the difficulty of discerning tone is through shorthand like "LOL" or the use of "emojis" or "emoticons," using punctuation to show:

Happy :)
Sad :(

Or more complex feelings: ;) (winking), :P (tongue sticking out), and others that may cause confusion even as they intend to clarify. But while emojis can be a useful way to convey tone in some cases, they do not actually change or counteract the content of the message. **Sticking a smiley face or "LOL" at the end of an unkind message does not make it kind**.

A child who texts: "It was great to see you! :)" or "Sorry you're home sick today :(" is being relatively direct, and it is unlikely that anyone would misinterpret his or her intent. But texting "You're so ugly ;)" or "Nice shoes LOL" clearly comes across as mean, and "See you later :P" could mean just about anything. We need to communicate to our children that while written words can be misinterpreted without tone of voice or body language, tacking on positive emojis does not automatically make an unkind statement acceptable. While emojis can be fun, there really is no shortcut past the process of stopping, reading through a message, and considering how the other person will interpret the written words.

Of course, part of this equation is helping our children give the benefit of the doubt when they are reading messages from others. The most charitable assumption is not always the correct one, but taking a breath and reading through a message can help us all to think about what the person who wrote it probably meant. Some children do not actively try to hurt their friends, and the sender may have simply written without thinking. We can help our children learn to ask, **Is there any way this could be misinterpreted?** as well as, **Is it possible that I am misinterpreting this?**

In written communication it is inherently more difficult to determine intent; therefore we all need to be vigilant about what we write and compassionate about what we read. We need to think about what we are saying and how it might be perceived. When we receive something, we can try to use our best judgment or use the power of the "delete" button.

Strengthen Your Power

PART OF BUILDING resilience is learning what you have control over and what you do not. The written word is powerful, but it is important for our children to remember that they always have the power to delete. They always have the option to delete posts and messages that hurt them or make them uncomfortable, and they have the option to unfriend, unfollow, or block people who are being unkind or thoughtless. Most sites have settings where a user can prevent other people from posting on their personal pages at all. This is not foolproof. No one can alter what is said about them in spaces they do not control, but children can regain power by remembering they can unplug, walk away, unfollow, delete, or block.

In the freefall of Internet communication, the delete button is a parachute. We do not need to subject ourselves to anything that makes us feel bad, because stepping back from it, though psychologically difficult, is physically easy. Children need to get into the habit of hitting the delete button, especially on their own walls and pages. Their pages should be about things that inspire them and make them feel like their best selves. They have control over that aspect of their environment, and in taking that power and using it, they can build resilience.

Does It Need to Be Said?

CRUELTY AND HARASSMENT are the darkest and most visible negative outcomes of ubiquitous social media, but they are a part of a larger culture—a culture where everything is shared, all the time, with one's entire social network, which is often their entire school. This, like so much of online culture, is not unique to children—many of us have that friend who posts pictures of every meal she eats, or that cousin who offers constant updates on his cat's daily activities. But for children, who are still learning to navigate the offline (or "real") world, learning how much is safe to share can be treacherous. My concern is that they may be learning both voyeuristic and narcissistic behaviors.

This is why I believe teaching privacy is so very important. Many of our children are constantly sharing updates on their lives, activities, thoughts, and feelings. Thinking, processing, and even writing about all of these things can be healthy and positive. Many of us grew up writing in diaries, but we did not post them publicly. The danger for a child in posting every thought and feeling he or she has is twofold: there is what children post about themselves and what they post about others. As we know, information a child shares about him or herself is publicly visible, and permanent. An emotional outburst posted late one night after an upsetting day might later be used against the child who shared it. Making oneself emotionally vulnerable in public offers fodder to other children who might misuse the information or use it to make fun of the child who shared their feelings. In any time period, and at any age, there are people who like to create drama, and the public forum of social media makes this easier than ever. Children who expose their own vulnerabilities are making themselves potential targets.

We have talked about teaching children to remember that the Internet personas of others do not show the whole story of who they are. But it is also important for them to understand that this is not entirely a bad thing. They have the power to shape their online persona and decide what piece of the story they will choose to present to the world.

This does not mean cutting and pasting only their most glamorous moments, or trying to create an online story in which their lives are flawless. What it does mean is that not every moment needs to be shared with everyone. It does not mean trying to present a perfect life. It simply means recognizing that some things are not meant for the whole world to see. Learning to build relationships and share your innermost feelings and thoughts with only those who you hold dear is special and emotionally healthy. This may guide our children away from feeding into voyeuristic or narcissistic behavior.

Regardless of how much a child shares about themselves, the other concern is what they choose to share about others. When children share every thought and feeling they have about someone else, the tone rarely stays positive or constructive and tends to be judgmental. Even when the intent is not to insult or attack another child but simply to express one's own frustration, posting something publicly may turn into an act of aggression. Many of us have heard, or possibly said, "If you don't have anything nice to say, don't say anything at all!" Maybe we need to update this for the new millennium, saying, "If you don't have anything nice to post, don't post anything at all."

"It is not my business what everyone thinks of me," is a good saying. For teenagers, whose social world is so fraught, it can feel like their whole life depends on what everyone thinks of them and what they think of everyone else. But sharing those opinions with an entire social network can only do harm and even lead to real cruelty. As parents, we can help our children to pause before they post, and ask themselves, **Is this anyone's business but**

my own? Or should this be shared only with someone who is close to me and truly cares about me?

The habit of sharing everything can also lead to safety issues offline. I do not understand why many adults share what they share, such as private and intimate thoughts and frustrations. But even more surprising are things like vacation plans. When I was growing up we were taught never to tell a caller on the phone that our parents were not home, so that no one would know we were alone and potentially vulnerable. If someone went out of town for a week, they did not spread the word to everyone they knew, and they made arrangements to have their mail and newspapers held, so it would not be obvious that the house was an easy target for a robbery. These days, we have gotten so accustomed to sharing every detail of our lives and plans online that it seems like it would be very easy for someone to plan a crime spree among their acquaintances. Check online to see who is going to be out of town and help yourself.

For children and teens, this kind of sharing can be even riskier, because they are so frequently indiscriminate about whom they allow into their online friend circles. Over and over I have heard this story: a teen's parents are going out of town and tell the child they can have a few friends over. The child texts three friends and invites them for the evening. Those friends text others, and then without warning, the house is filled with hundreds of kids, and the child cannot get them out. Because there are so many people in the house, and because they have no real connection to the unwitting host, the party gets out of control; there may be drinking, and possessions may be destroyed. One girl I spoke with ended up calling her mother's friend and begging for help to get everyone out of the house.

Even without invitations being sent out, just the knowledge that a house is empty can create opportunities for mischief. One parent told me that word had gotten out that her family was going out of town. A group of teens found out and began using her backyard as a place to drink and hang out because they thought they would be unobserved. In this case, they were spotted by a neighbor and sent away, but the owners of the house were rightly concerned that underage drinking was going on, on their property. We need to make sure our children realize that the information they post online can be seen by just about anyone. If they would not tell a stranger on the street their home address, they should not post it online. If they cannot trust their friends to keep invitations to themselves, then maybe they should invite someone who can be discreet.

Offline Consequences

WHILE IT IS tempting to think of the online and offline worlds as separate, "virtual reality" versus "actual reality," we need to begin to see both as equally impactful aspects of the world our children inhabit. Though computers can be turned off and phones stashed away, the conversations, sharing, and even harassment that happen online are happening in reality, and too often, they are inescapable. When children are unable to get away from rumors and attacks that are happening online, the consequences are far-reaching or sometimes horrifying and tragic.

Schools are now dealing with children who are reluctant to come to school because of posts made about them online; some children have been so badly humiliated and harassed via the Internet that they are on suicide watch, have made suicide attempts, or have ended their lives. We, as parents and educators, need to do a better job in guiding our children to use technology with good intent.

One of the things I have heard about time and again at the schools I visit is the fallout when a couple breaks up. Often this is the first relationship—and the first heartbreak—for both children. When a child's heart is broken for the first time, they will often reach out online for comfort, or for vindication. They might post mean and hurtful things about the other person, or pour out their pain for everyone to see, sometimes dragging everyone they know into their private fight. Sometimes, information that was shared during the relationship becomes fodder for a public conflict, which raises the question, how much responsibility do we have for another person's privacy after a relationship has ended?

Young people's frequent lack of concern for their own privacy can extend to the privacy of others. But we need to teach our children that when you have a private relationship with someone, you have to maintain the privacy afterward. Because they are so used to sharing every thought and feeling they have, it can be hard for them to realize that sharing someone else's intimate thoughts and feelings is truly a violation of someone's privacy. Children who take the pain of their breakups to social media may start conflicts that tear their friend groups apart, instead of retreating to lick their wounds in private. They may hurt their ex-partners terribly by lashing out publicly, or they may open themselves up to attack, simply by putting their pain on display for everyone they know to see. Part of growing up is learning emotional self-regulation. Children must learn to manage emotions, even terribly painful ones, with respect for others and for themselves.

We need to teach our children to take their feelings and their hurt offline, to the people who truly care about them. This is what our friends are for, at all ages—to support us and help us through the rough times in our lives, as well as to share in the joyous moments. As we discussed in the previous chapter, sharing emotions and reaching out is vitally important, but it is just as important for our children to consider with whom they are sharing. One of the lessons of friendship is that while it feels good to have people care about you, not everyone will, and private information and private thoughts are only for the people who do. This is normal—privacy is not the same as keeping a secret, and it does not mean that what is private is bad. For our children, being mindful of their privacy just means stopping to think before sharing, and asking, **Is this any of this person's business?**

Mindful Words

WE NEED TO teach our children that words have power. Regardless of intention, the things they write about themselves and about one another can have lasting consequences. We need to guide our children to write with good intent, but we also need to help them step back, be mindful, and consider the impact of their words, and pause before they post, by asking themselves these questions:

» **Would I say what I've typed face to face? (Kindness)**
» **Would this make me feel good if I received it? (Empathy)**
» **Is my text clear without misunderstanding? (Perception)**
» **Is this post a reflection of the true person I am? (Intent)**
» **Is this personal/private? Does it need to be shared? (Privacy)**
» **Am I spreading negativity? (Eeyore)**

The last question brings me to the social media "Eeyore," the person who is always posting about their mopey mood, about the bad weather, the terrible traffic, or hinting vaguely at drama behind the curtain. "Don't you hate rainy days?" "Some people need to learn to mind their own business." "Mondays are the worst," and so on. We all have frustrations and challenges in our lives, and it is easy to express that on social media, seeking commiseration, and it is easy to respond to, because most of us can relate to those daily disappointments. For me, seeing a long string of negativity affects my mood, even when it is not directed at me. When we focus on the negative, we are making a choice to notice the things that bring us down, and to make the things that upset us the story of our day. Every time we share something upsetting or jump on someone else's negative bandwagon, we reinforce that negative energy. Use your power to delete, unfollow, or block.

But what if we taught our children to use the power of social media for good? We can see how powerfully even a minor negative comment can affect a child. How much of an impact would it have for a child to see random acts of kindness posted on their social media pages? We see children seeking approval and attention through negative means online, but there is truly no reason they cannot find those things through more positive routes.

Because words are so powerful and can be seen by so many, children can learn to use them in positive ways. Even if children do make mistakes, which they all will, and write something unkind publicly, they can easily apologize publicly. Making amends would lessen the blow the next day at school, both for the child who made the post and for the child targeted. An apology might even make other students stop and think before they write something. This might make the difference between a child not wanting to attend school and being able to hold their head up high.

In my community we have incorporated a Social Media Challenge day, which encourages children to use social media in positive ways. Perhaps your child's school or community would like to pose a similar challenge, asking your children to spend the day using their technology in only a kind and careful manner. You might suggest some things children can post publicly to spread positivity among their friend groups. Some examples are:

» Send a funny joke.
» Write something nice about someone who you know could use a boost.
   I thought you did great at try outs, keep working at it and you'll make it next year.
» Send a kind text.
   I love your sweater, where'd you get it?
» Share a positive or inspiring quote.
   It is nice to be important, but it is more important to be nice.—Unknown
» Send a silly picture of yourself.
» Express a positive thing about your day and why it made you happy.
   I wish I could live this day over again. Everything went right! Just passed my road test.
» Text an apology to someone you hurt because it has been weighing heavily on your mind.
   I am so sorry that I excluded you from my party last year.
» Compliment a classmate.
   You make me feel welcome at your lunch table. Thank you!

It is hard enough out there, especially for young people struggling to find their way in the world; they do not need to make it harder for themselves. We can encourage our children to look for and share the positive in their lives; to think back over their day and focus on the things that made them feel happy, or proud, even if those things are small. We can help them to post what they are excited about, not what they are angry about; to form the habits of posting compliments and sharing things they are proud of. Words do have power— we need to remember that they have the power to uplift, to spread kindness and positive energy. We can help our children to be mindful and to post with positive intent. For many children, the last thing they do before going to bed is check their social media pages and chat with their friends. Imagine the impact if they were to make a conscious decision to end each day with positivity, as we all should. That's why I tape *The Ellen DeGeneres Show* every night and watch it before I go to sleep. It is a positive, funny, feel-good show that ends my day with the right attitude.

CHAPTER FOUR
Cell Phones

» What is communication?

Communication is the process of getting information from one person to another.

MY CHILDREN, LIKE most of my peers' children, were given a cell phone somewhere around the time of middle school. For my family, that was sixth grade, around eleven years old. Looking back, I am not proud to say that I didn't give much thought to giving my children this device. I believe I had succumbed to parental peer pressure and began to believe that giving my children a cell phone as they entered middle school was a rite of passage. Many parents state that this is a good time to give them a cell phone, because they begin to have more freedom, and a cell phone enables parents to keep in touch and know their children's whereabouts. I am still on the fence about whether that is allowing our children room to grow and gain independence or if it is giving them a false sense of it. At this time, it feels a little Big Brotherish to me. I have seen this ability to track their children cause parents to become too involved and to feel overly responsible for their children's actions. As an educator, I know it is important to allow our children to make mistakes and learn from them. I have witnessed some pretty remarkable educational and, even more so, emotional, growth happen when we allow this to take place. I was taught to provide children with the opportunity to build resilience and perseverance by allowing them to make mistakes. As I have seen my students' growth, I have pointed out to them the ways in which they have changed and progressed. Saying things like, "Look what you've accomplished, and look what you can be," will help children to own their accomplishments. Unfortunately, I have also seen a child being pigeonholed as "bad" by parents and teachers, which has the negative effect on children, creating a self-fulfilling prophecy. We must recognize that our children will both succeed and fail, and we must teach them to handle both appropriately.

Letting go and allowing the ups and downs to arise is not an easy thing to do, most likely because we are much more emotionally connected and invested. However, we have to allow for these natural moments to arise and to become teachable moments for our children. Simple, but not easy. This is where we, as adults, draw on what personally helps us. For me, my faith, my friends, my family, and mindful meditation helps me to relinquish control and allow my children to grow. Today, technology adds another challenge for us as parents. If we allow ourselves to be overly connected to our children by using these devices, we may be getting in the way of their journey. As we know, this is the most difficult but necessary part of parenting—allowing our children to make their own mistakes.

When we give our children a cell phone we are not just giving them a communication device. A cell phone has the capacity for much more. It provides access to the Internet, video and photo capability, and the ability to download apps, all of which allow little parental control. Not all apps are age-appropriate, yet they are very easily downloaded. This means we have to realize that we may be giving our child something that he or she may or may not be mature enough to handle. It has become obvious that many of us have not properly educated or prepared our children for this responsibility. Providing our children with guidelines and strategies will empower them and, in turn, may lessen their anxiety. As I mentioned in the introduction, parents have to take ownership of our actions. We hand over cell phones without a thought, as though they were toys, when the reality is that they contain everything a child needs to seriously damage their own future or that of another child. We are giving them these devices, yet we did not equip them with the tools, or in many cases the maturity, to properly use them. It is our parental responsibility to create those guidelines, to talk them through with our children *before* we give them their own personal technology, to set a good example, and to help them navigate well. Downloading the Don't Press Send app and reviewing the Pledge from time to time will remind our children of the importance of kind and careful communication.

At every workshop, I ask students, "When you got your cell phone, what rules did your parents give you?" Most children say, "Don't lose it, don't break it." In workshops from third grade through high school, most students report that there was little to no discussion regarding guidelines, besides taking responsibility for the actual device itself.

Healthy Habits

WHEN WE MAKE the decision to give our children access to technology, we may think of safety and convenience first. Having a cell phone means we can be in touch about rides and carpooling, and that children can let us know when they are running late. Cell phones save us some serious worry, when a child can call from a party that has become rowdy or unsafe to get a ride home. Only second do we think about the disadvantages that obviously now occur to us: Will he or she spend too much time talking to friends? Will they give their numbers to acquaintances, who may not be trustworthy? But many of the challenges that come with cell phones were things that I did not consider, largely because I had no idea they existed. Early cell phones were just that— phones. But these days they are essentially hand-held computers, with all the risks and benefits that entails.

The greatest attraction of the cell phone is also its greatest challenge: it goes everywhere its owner goes. This is the point, and it has made things like meeting friends, updating schedules, and finding out who will be home for dinner so much easier. When we were growing up, being late coming home from school or a night out could cause a great deal of concern for our parents, but if our children want to go out after classes, or get a flat tire coming home from a date, they can let us know immediately. They can summon roadside assistance if they are in an accident, or even call 911 in the event of emergency. Equipping our children with phones is, in many ways, a safety precaution. But, there are also dangers inherent in giving a child around-the-clock Internet access.

Giving our children guidelines for cell phone use means considering some of the obstacles they can run into, as well as setting some limits on the use of the device itself. When the cell phone is always there, it means our children are never truly free to be fully present to where they are and what they are supposed to be doing. If studying is constantly interrupted by text messages, how do they concentrate? If they are checking for "likes" and replies to a post, how can they relax enough to go to sleep? Some things that we can encourage, or even mandate, are **cell phone–free hours for homework and a set time for docking the phone in the evening**. No child needs their cell phone next to their bed when they should be sleeping. A better choice might be to **buy an alarm clock and not get in the habit of using the cell phone as an alarm**. It has become the norm that our children's phones are often the last thing they see before they go to bed and the first thing they check as soon as they wake. Maybe we need to rethink what we have accepted as commonplace.

Beyond building healthy habits for using their phones, we also need to help our children to recognize the risks they can open themselves up to when they are not careful with their personal information. As early as fourth grade, I have found that children share passwords and account information with one another in order to play games on each other's phones and computers. Among college students, it is common for someone who finds a friend's device unlocked to send messages or photos from that friend's account. Though sharing games and playing pranks may seem harmless, there is always a risk involved. What may seem like a joke posted to a friend's Twitter account may damage their reputation or create an impression that cannot be undone. If the prankster resorts to bullying someone else, it will be all but impossible to prove that the account holder was not the one who posted. Sharing gaming passwords may seem harmless, but it gets children in the habit of treating password and account information as though it is not strictly private, which can lead to bad habits with more serious consequences. Even if a child is "only" sharing a password to a gaming or movie-streaming site with a trusted friend, they need to ask, **Can they trust the friend not to share it with someone else?**

Additionally, paid accounts for gaming or video streaming may provide access to credit card information, or address information, that should be kept private under all circumstances. And while we should all use distinct passwords for every website, children who provide the password to their gaming account then use the same password for their private email or bank statement may be setting themselves up for serious harm. Our children need to get in the habit of treating personal information as private and never to be shared.

Taking Pictures

CELL PHONES GO everywhere our children go, which means they rarely have a phone-free moment, and indeed little, if any, time for them to be disconnected from their entire social circle. When do children get to be bored? When can they daydream or have time to clear their minds and be creative? Is it any wonder that our best ideas come when we are in the shower, when we are completely disconnected?

Cell phones are our children's primary means of communication—even outstripping that old-fashioned tradition of talking face-to-face. Because they have cell phones all the time, they have become accustomed to acting on every impulse. Many times children text on impulse and give very little time for a thoughtful response.

As parents, we are sometimes the ones setting a bad example. How many times have we asked our children to pose for pictures before an event, then rushed to post them online? It is not that we should not take photos—after all, it is nice to have a physical reminder of a memory—but when our children focus exclusively on taking the picture and posting it, when do they have time to actually enjoy the party, game, or event? When we insist on documenting every second of life, we are unknowingly discouraging mindfulness. We need to encourage our children to take photos of things they want to remember, but then to put the phone away and enjoy the moment they are in, not spend the whole day obsessing about what it will look like later and who will view or "like" it.

Our insistence on photographing and sharing everything—places, events, accomplishments, and even our meals—promotes a mindset in which every-thing our children do is overshadowed by the desire to record it, post online, and garner "likes" or followers. When I was young, my parents taught me that boasting and bragging were rude and not to be done; the culture of sharing and posting about every little thing seems to me to run counter to that dictum. Even as adults, it is easy to get into a game of one-upmanship, posting photos of our most glamorous or exciting moments every chance we get. It is no wonder that our children are doing the same thing. Once again, it feeds into narcissistic behavior.

Not only does the focus on taking and posting pictures take time and energy away from whatever the event is supposed to be, it sets up a competitive and exclusionary dynamic among the children there and, worse, the children not there. Sharing photos taken at a party with the other children who were present is one thing. But the way our children are sharing photos is public— simply publishing them to a profile page for everyone to see. This means that everything they post is visible to their entire friend circle, both the friends who were invited to the party and those who were not invited. Because the photos are public, it is not only that a child will feel left out, realizing that he or she is not part of the group, but also that his or her exclusion will be public. Not only were they not invited, but everyone knows they were not invited—this can be a source of public humiliation. As parents, we may not think about it from this angle, until it is our own child who is being excluded, but maybe we should be thinking more globally and reinforce our children's empathetic skills. Maybe we should think of cyber civics.

Throughout my presentations, adults also have shared stories with me about the hurt of exclusion. One teacher told me about her own story of exclusion. She had a group of neighborhood friends who were accustomed to spending a lot of time together during the week. Though she was somewhat newer to the group than the others, she felt equally welcomed and liked, and she considered these women to be close friends. Then one day, after a long weekend, she saw photos posted to their social media pages of a winery trip they had all taken—without her. She was hurt and felt left out and even deliberately excluded. Though she tried to ignore it—after all, they had been friends with each other longer than with her—she found that their friendship had changed. She felt betrayed, and her relationships with what had once been close friends cooled and became strained. In fact, the group had done nothing wrong by not inviting her. Not everyone gets invited to everything, whether because some gatherings are smaller than others or just because some friends are closer than others. But social media force those who have been excluded to see what they have missed, and what may be a normal part of social life can feel like a deliberate slight or snub that is done publicly. Plainly and simply, **what people don't know won't hurt them**. By not documenting and posting, you can avoid hurting someone's feelings.

This is not to say that children should never take or share pictures, only that they need to be mindful about who they are sharing them with. A good rule of thumb is to **share photos only with the other people who were there when the photo was taken, or who are in the photo themselves**. Another good habit to get into is **asking others not to re-post with "#PNRP" (Please No Reposting)**.

We have discussed in previous chapters how important it is for children to understand that glamorous photos posted online do not tell the whole story of another person's life. We also need to teach them to stop before they post pictures and think about how they will come across to others. Children need to ask themselves, **Am I posting this just to boast? Who am I excluding? Am I seeking "likes"?**

Another question that I feel is important is, **Do I have permission to post this photo?** We have reached a point culturally where it is common, and even considered normal, for photos to be taken at any gathering and then immediately posted online. As an adult, I know a number of serial posters who share dozens of photos from every event they attend, pictures in which by some miracle they always look fantastic, while I often seem to be blinking or tilting my head at a medically impossible angle, showing my five chins. I do not appreciate someone posting pictures of me whether I look good or bad. It is a personal preference of what I want shared—for example, who I am with and where I am is not for public knowledge.

Recently I went to Charleston with a group of twelve girlfriends for my friend's fiftieth birthday. I firmly believe that from time to time I need to take off my "mom hat" and let my hair down. We were walking and saw people dancing in street, so we joined in enthusiastically. After a few moments, I noticed a kid filming us. Putting my "mom hat" back on, I walked up to him and said, "Why are you filming us?"

"It's no big deal," he said.

"It is," I said. "You have video of me and my friends, and I don't want you to. Please delete it."

I don't know if he did, but the incident upset me. It is as though the whole world has become paparazzi and we are all living like stars, without the multimillion-dollar contracts. I am human and I like to have fun and let my hair down; this does not mean I am not responsible, but the image of fifty-year-old women having fun instead of driving to soccer practice could easily be taken out of context and damage my image as a responsible educator and parent. That young man had no right to take a video of me, but there was nothing I could do to stop it.

A person's image is their own, and it is an important thing. There is a reason that models are paid for what they do, and there is a reason that we as parents have to sign release forms before our children's schools can use their photographs for any promotional or educational materials. My image, like my name, is worth something to me. I should have the right to control, or at least have a say in, where it ends up.

Recently I received two invitations to two different places at the same time. Because I lack the power to be in two places at once, I told one person I couldn't go and went to other party. However, at the party I went to, someone was taking pictures and tagged me in several photos, which I was unaware of. They then posted the pictures on social media. Through the network of "friends of friends," the person whose invitation I had declined saw this photo and "liked" it. Now I know that she saw it, and I imagine her feelings must have been hurt to see that I chose another party over hers. This was never my intention. I had to choose one place to go, and it was not hers, and had my picture not been shared, that would have been fine. But the friend who posted my photo forced her to see what I was doing instead. In our culture, posting and sharing images of other people has become commonplace, but we can teach our children to be more respectful of the boundaries of others. Just as we teach them not to share private information entrusted to them by their friends without asking, we can teach them to ask permission before taking a photo and ask permission again before posting it online. Although generally, the only consequence of sharing a photo of someone else is embarrassment or discomfort, there are many times when photo sharing is far, far more serious.

Compromising Positions

WE HAVE ALL heard the story: a girl takes photos of herself without clothing on and sends them to her boyfriend. The boyfriend shares them with his friends. Soon, the whole school has seen them, and the girl is being so terribly harassed that she stops coming to school. Because most of the harassment takes place online, she cannot get away from it. There have been children who attempted to take their own lives over this and children who have actually committed suicide. It is horrifying, and even worse, it is common. Some of these stories have made the national news, particularly when they involve a death, but the reality is that they happen everywhere, and far too often. I can think of several cases off the top of my head, cases involving school districts I have spoken at and others nearby. Sometimes it is photos shared around the school and sometimes it is videos of children performing sexual acts. Sometimes the participants both know they are being filmed; sometimes one or both of them are unaware. The cruelty and the damage surrounding these scenarios is awful and sometimes irreversible because of the permanency and the sheer number of people it reaches.

At one school where I spoke, they were dealing with precisely this situation. A seventh-grade girl had given photos of herself without her clothing on to her boyfriend, sending them via cell phone. The boyfriend had asked for them, and, trusting him, she sent them. Immediately, he showed them and sent them to some of his friends. The girl was humiliated to an unimaginable level. She had been on suicide watch and became reluctant to go to school, which caused her to eventually switch schools. Children who have put themselves in this compromising position are often forced to deal with problems that are wildly beyond their age, things that would be horrible for a twenty-year-old, never mind a 13-year-old. Many children in this position develop school phobias and trust issues. One of my beliefs for every human being on this planet, big or small, is that one incident does not define the whole person. Unfortunately, because of the permanency of the Internet and everything on it, many children who have posted something that they are ashamed of end up requiring intensive therapy to strengthen their feelings of self-worth. Some children even end up choosing to change schools because the humiliation is so great, and because it takes time to overcome. But if the photos or videos surface online, which they may if the child's name is attached, the nightmare can begin all over again. I know that I made mistakes when I was young that were humiliating to me, but over time they were forgotten. The permanent and public nature of the Internet means that our children are facing consequences far out of proportion with the immature errors they make.

This generation is far from the first to shame young adults for their sexual behavior, or even their presumed sexual behavior. When we were in middle and high school there were rumors about this child or that, doing this thing or that, but they were always rumors. Documented proof was rare. Now, instead of a boy bragging to his friends about a conquest, or an adolescent trying to find his sexual identity, a claim that might be believed or not can be proven, and within seconds, everyone in the entire school can see for themselves.

It is easy, perhaps, to say that these tragedies could be avoided if children did not behave in ways that they wouldn't want broadcast around the school. We can teach our children the values we want them to live by, and we can teach them to protect themselves. But the reality is, they will make mistakes, just as we made mistakes when we were their age. Right now, some of our children are paying for their mistakes publicly with consequences that are wildly out of proportion to their actions. Most of us have trusted the wrong person; we have all done something that seemed like a good idea at the time. We have all caved to peer pressure, whether it was taking a dare in high school, trying drugs and alcohol, or even taking the same sexual risks we see children taking today. But the consequences were limited, and the embarrassment faded as people forgot, and we moved on to the next thing. Today, the crime does not fit the punishment.

With cell phones, the misjudgments our children make can be recorded and posted to the Internet, and as we know, anything on the Internet is both public and permanent. Certainly, we need to teach our children not to engage sexually with each other at such a young age. But as much as we need to talk to them about sexual behavior, we need to talk to them about technology. Right now we may be giving them technological tools they are not yet mature enough to use responsibly, and we may not be providing them with the guidelines that they so desperately need. I gave my children cell phones from the time they were in sixth grade, and I now know that they were not ready to use them responsibly. They have been fortunate, as far as I know. Our children need to understand that once they send a picture or video of themselves to someone else, it is out of their control. "Nothing is private." Even if they think they can trust the recipient, the consequences of being wrong can be immense.

It's the Law

CHILDREN WHO SEND around photos and videos of their peers without clothing on or doing inappropriate or sexual things may think that their actions are no big deal. But just as the consequences can be far-reaching for the victims of this kind of harassment, they can be terrible for the perpetrators as well.

Legally, child pornography is defined as *any* sexual or inappropriate images of minors, no matter how they were obtained, or by whom. This means that even photos or videos taken and shared by other minors could count as child pornography. It means that even a child who takes photos or videos of **him- or herself** without clothes on could be technically guilty of making and distributing child pornography. This is something most children (and many parents) are unaware of, and it is something that can have far-reaching consequences.

One situation I was told about during the course of my speaking engagements was a girl who had taken photos of herself without clothes on and sent them to her boyfriend. He had then sent them to his friends, who started sharing them around the school. The girl did the courageous thing and told her father what had happened. Naturally, he was furious at the young men, and he reported their actions to the police. The boys were indeed questioned by the police. However, because his daughter had taken the photos and been the first to distribute them, she too was questioned by the police. Because of the ways the laws surrounding child pornography are written, the child who takes pictures or videos of him or herself is just as liable as other children who distribute them. The penalties for possession and distribution of child pornography are harsh, and while it may be unlikely that minors would be prosecuted for distributing pictures of themselves to other minors, some older teenagers have found themselves on the Sex Offender Registry following the consensual exchange of photographs and videos. I recall a news story of a nineteen-year-old Florida man whose girlfriend was fourteen, meaning that their relationship violated Florida's consent laws. They broke up, and the young man shared photos and videos of her with sexual content. The girl's family decided to prosecute, and because she was a minor, he is now on the sex offender list. This is a designation that will follow children around for years, decades, or even the rest of their lives and can affect their educations, future job prospects, and even where they are allowed to live. Whether or not we consider these laws just, we need to make our children well aware of the potential penalties they may face for what can seem like simple experimentation.

There are also consequences to schools as a whole when children act out in these ways. In a previous chapter, I discussed New York State's Dignity for All Students Act, which requires New York schools to report to the state any incidents of bullying, intimidation, or harassment among students, whether it takes place on or off school property. This law has a number of implications, one of which is simply that we as a society are taking bullying and harassment far more seriously than we have in the past. Schools are required to take action in these cases, which means that there are more likely to be consequences for engaging in inappropriate and hostile behavior than when we were growing up. This may mean punishment, like detention, suspension, and even expulsion, or it may mean notation of the behavior on a student's permanent record, a consequence that can follow them to college and beyond. It also means that schools are forced to spend time and resources investigating even incidents that happen off school property and not during school hours.

Recently I was made aware of yet another incident involving students sharing a compromising video, which occurred over a weekend. On Monday, the school was notified, and the administration spent hours sorting out what had happened and reporting it to the appropriate authorities. While the principle of taking student harassment seriously at a state level is a good one, it seems unbalanced that the burden of reporting and discipline should fall to schools, which should be spending their time and energy educating our children. Schools alone cannot be the only place we look to when it comes to educating our children on good cyber citizenship. I worry that schools may be expected to devote too much of their scarce resources to discipline problems that occur beyond their scope and off their property. Maybe parents and schools could share the balance and partner up as we educate our children. I believe most schools will tell you that they spend far too many hours dealing with cyber incidents. Maybe if parents and schools together educate and empower our children to be more cyber-civically responsible, we will have fewer incidents in and around our communities.

Many of us have said, "I don't understand the technology," and that is to some extent fair. "Kids today" are using multiple platforms and programs, and by the time you finish reading this book, they will be using new and different ones. But teaching our children how to behave while using technology does not require us to understand every site they use. We need to teach them rules for how they engage with one another, whether it is online, at school, or at the beach. Regardless of the communication medium, those rules should be the same. "I don't understand technology" may be true, but it cannot be an excuse for failing to teach children online respect. We can help them to form "civil cyber communities," even if we are not intimately engaged in the "cyber" part of things.

Addiction

CELL PHONES CAN be everywhere we are, and everyone who has our number knows where to find us, all the time. Over the last decade, multiple studies and articles have examined the fact that American workers are seeing more and more comingling of their work time with their leisure time. When we are at home we are connected to work, and when we are at work, we are connected to our home responsibilities. Because we are always available, whether with our families or our colleagues, we begin to feel like we have to be in touch. The time when we could excuse a missed call by saying, "I was out of the house" has long since passed.

I know that when I do not answer my phone, because I am driving, busy with something else, or simply because I do not feel like answering the phone at the moment, people get annoyed with me. Some even take it as a personal affront if I do not immediately return calls or text messages. In reality, I am simply taking care of the priorities in my life. The expectation of availability can leave us anxious and feeling like we have to constantly check our devices.

One thing we can do to help our children unplug is to grant one another a bit more flexibility, to not expect an immediate response from others, and to not feel like each call, text, or email is a summons that cannot be ignored. The way we treat our phones, as though their demands take precedence above all else, cannot be healthy. On the one hand, we interrupt whatever we were doing when the call comes—time with our families, work, or simply relaxing.

Leaping to answer the phone means the time we were spending doing something else is interrupted and unfocused. On the other hand, if we are busy with something when the call comes, our response will be hurried and not thoughtful. We will not be taking the time to engage with whoever is on the other end of the line. Pushing ourselves to focus on one thing at a time can give us the ability to put our attention on each thing we do, instead of trying to do it all at once. From this action, we can learn to become more mindful.

I believe that cell phones are addictive, by any definition of the word. My teenage son had developed a habit of doing his homework with his cell phone sitting right next to him as he worked. Every few minutes, he would get a text alert and drop what he was doing to respond. Concerned for his ability to concentrate, I took his phone away for the remaining eight weeks of the semester, hoping this would give him some time to get into a healthier study pattern. Other parents thought this was draconian; I thought it was perfectly reasonable. As the weeks passed, I began to be seriously concerned that my son was falling into a depression—he was, I believe, going through withdrawal. His friends, a creative and funny bunch, went as far as to make up shirts that said #ConnectMichael.

The addictive nature of the phone makes sense, in context. Like slot machines, they dole out intermittent rewards, even beeping and blinking when you have a new message. The pressure to immediately respond makes it difficult to focus on anything but when the next reply will come, and it makes all communication feel urgent and important. Children feel like they can't stand to miss anything; they keep their phones with them at all times, even when they should be focused on something else.

The need to be constantly connected is more than a simple habit. When children receive "likes" or comments on something they posted, the pleasure center of the brain lights up. Soon, even the act of posting something in anticipation of those "likes" has the same effect. No wonder they want to keep doing it! Their brain is responding to it the way it would to any addictive behavior.

Some children even sleep with their phones nearby, getting up in the middle of the night if they hear an alert. They sleep poorly, with constant interruptions, and some will even get up, half awake, in the night to respond to a text, then go back to sleep and wake up with no memory of having sent the message. There have even been cases of cell phones catching on fire in a child's bed. This is extreme, of course, but when we allow cell phones to have such a place of primacy in our own lives, it is hardly surprising that our children will do the same.

A friend of mine recently decided to institute cell phone–free hours after 9:00 p.m. He had noticed that his teenage children were on their phones all night, and in an effort to bring a healthier balance into their lives, he asked them to hand over their phones in the evening. His ninth-grade daughter rolled her eyes but gave him the phone. He told me he thought she was even a little bit relieved to be able to detach from the constant social network. His son, in eleventh grade, however, reacted more strongly. He argued and yelled, insisting that he had never done anything wrong with his cell phone. My friend told me it was like using the Ferber method with his son all over again, leaving him alone to cry himself to sleep. As a mom, I remember how torn I felt letting my children cry as they learned to self-soothe; it goes against every natural instinct to stand by while your baby screams bloody murder. But our children who have become overly attached to their phones may need a digital detox, and giving it to them is, ultimately, a service.

Mindful Communication

RECENTLY I WAS at the gym early in the morning, and the only other woman in the room with me was talking loudly on her cell phone, distracting me from my exercise and my thoughts, even after I had put on headphones in the hope of drowning her out. When eventually I asked her to please speak more quietly or take the call outside, she replied,

"No one is here."

I was there! She told me about all the problems she was trying to deal with, and that this was an extremely important call, and I tried to be calm and kind and express that I was sorry, but we all have problems and stresses, and I come to the gym to get away from my own.

Frequently, I see cashiers in the checkout line, desk clerks, and other workers on the job talking or texting on their phones while performing customer service tasks. The tasks themselves suffer, but besides that, it is rude and instills a poor work ethic. By not paying attention to what they are doing, they are communicating to me, the customer, that they do not care about doing their job well. Even if they are perfectly able to text with one hand and type with the other, the perception of the person watching them is that they may become unemployable and exhibit disrespectful behavior. I do not want the person making a transaction with me to be focused elsewhere while we interact, just like I do not want my children's teachers to be posting pictures of their last dinner party in the middle of their lessons, or playing Candy Crush. I would not want my accountant distracted while calculating my taxes, and I would not want my surgeon to be checking text messages while removing my appendix!

That last example sounds like an exaggeration, but something similar happened to me. Back in 2001, I was giving birth to my twins and required a C-section. Because of a heart condition, I needed careful monitoring while undergoing anesthesia. During the operation, I was given local anesthetic and a sedative, but I was still awake and aware. As I prepared for my children to come into the world, I heard the anesthesiologist on the phone . . . ordering her lunch!

I had chosen the hospital because of its excellent reputation; I was about to go through one of the most important moments in my life, and to this day I can remember what my anesthesiologist had for lunch (a grilled chicken Caesar salad with dressing on the side and a Diet Coke, if you're wondering). I was fine, and my twins were fine, but the disrespect, unprofessionalism, and catastrophic potential of this event shocks me to this day.

Constant State of Distraction

WHEN WE ARE multitasking, we are simply not able to work to the best of our abilities. When I was a teenager, I borrowed my father's car one night and accidentally left a McDonald's bag on the backseat. When he discovered it, he summoned me out to the car to talk to me. I thought I would be in trouble for leaving a mess in his car, but that is not what he began the conversation with. He very sternly asked me if I had been eating or drinking while driving. He stated that I was to have both hands on the wheel at all times. Not one french fry, not one sip of soda was to be had. Not paying attention for a split second could change my life or someone else's forever. He did ultimately get to his normal rant that leaving a mess was disrespecting other people's things. I believe that over the years, we have slowly come to accept the idea that it is acceptable and normal to drive while distracted. We eat and drink, we program our GPS, we put a CD into the player, or we reach into a purse to find something. We tell our children not to text and drive, but we often model distraction for them.

This division of attention is just as damaging in personal relationships, and it is almost nonsensical. With a real, live person in front of us, why would we give all our attention to people onscreen? Yet it happens, with couples in restaurants, children at the dinner table, or a driver texting. Just as our work suffers when we multitask, our relationships suffer when we are unable to give our full focus to the people we are with. Although we may be in constant contact, the overall effect is one of isolation. Multitasking also has long-term effects on a child's ability to focus and succeed in later life; children who do not learn to concentrate on one thing will not be able to give their work the full attention and effort it deserves, in school and later in life.

Instead of telling the people who truly care about our every triumph and defeat, we post to the whole world. Your grandmother truly cares what her granddaughter or grandson wore to their latest event—a Sweet Sixteen or a Bar Mitzvah—and wants to watch a video of your child playing or singing at a recital. Your distant acquaintances may not. By posting everything as a default, we may be sharing with people who are not invested in our lives and depriving those who are more invested of a more intimate contact. **As we engage in more low-quality communication, we lose out on high quality communication.**

Fundamentally, mindfulness is about respect. It is about respect for ourselves, respect for others, and respect for whatever it is we may be doing in the moment. The divided attention we give to our surroundings when we are constantly checking our phones for updates means that we are rarely fully present and cannot give our full self to the task at hand, be it work, leisure, or the companionship of another human being. There is a saying, "Jack of all trades, master of none," referring to someone who can do a number of things well but nothing with full competence. I worry that the culture of constant distraction is encouraging this tendency in our children, to never engage in anything with full concentration.

We can model mindful communication for our children by encouraging cell phone curfews, by not treating a phone call or a text alert as a summons, and by being present with our children when we are with them. We can teach them to ask, **What is the most important thing for me to focus on right now?**

CHAPTER FIVE
Peer Affirmation

» What is pride?

Pride is the feeling of self-respect and accomplishment attained through achievement.

» What is affirmation?

Affirmation is a positive reinforcement that strengthens your belief in yourself.

MANY OF US recall what it was like to be a teenager and desperate for acceptance. The desire to be accepted by one's community is not immature and it is not shallow. Although most of us will develop a stronger sense of self as we get older and be able to resist the pressures we want to resist, it is a reality that human beings need one another to survive. Ostracizing is a severe punishment, and cultures that practice shunning take it very seriously. Back at the dawn of our history, being excluded from the group would have meant being left to fend for oneself against the elements and against predators and would likely have resulted in death. Some teens are lured into cults, gangs, or now terrorist cells at this age, even children who come from stable homes. At an age when any parental strictures can feel too repressive, children are vulnerable to those who prey on their need to fit in. Children who seek the approval and acceptance of their peers are reacting to a real, primal fear. But we need to help them temper those reactions and discern when the price for that acceptance is too high, and give them the skills to build a stronger sense of self by reinforcing the notion of self-pride.

Teaching children to be emotionally self-reliant cannot happen overnight, but our thought patterns and mental processes can be shaped and molded, just like our physical bodies. A bodybuilder does not get strong overnight. He or she begins with a five-pound weight, then a ten-pound weight, and slowly and steadily progresses until he or she can lift a massive barbell above his or her head. We can help our children develop the muscles of self-pride, teaching them to ask themselves, **How did that make me feel? What will make me feel proud of myself?** We can teach them to rely on their inner strength and to place less importance on outside opinions.

"Everybody Is Doing It"

THE PHRASE "EVERYBODY'S doing it" is a cliché at this point, but when it comes to social media, "everybody" really *is* doing it. When almost everyone around you is doing something, it becomes easy to see that as the norm, even when that norm is harmful. Unkind social media are not in the same category as using drugs or drinking, activities children know are dangerous but do anyway in order to gain social cachet or test their own limits. Widespread social media use is simply the reality. However, *how* it is used needs to be evaluated by all. Children who spend all day on their phones are not rebelling; they are just living their lives, doing what "everybody" is doing.

They need to dissect the difference between harmful versus helpful, kind versus unkind, healthy attachment versus unhealthy attachment.

The call of "everybody is doing it" can be powerful even to adults. As I mentioned in an earlier chapter, part of the reason I gave my children cell phones so early was because, well, all the other moms were doing it. This was the norm of my peer group, and I am not proud, but I must be honest and admit that I did not fully interrogate my decision outside of that context. More power to the parents who say "no" to social media, but that is not my reality. My concern is how we are using it. As parents, we need to encourage our children to question the decisions they are making on social media. Part of resisting peer pressure is learning to be mindful about our choices, and learning to ask before we act, **Why am I doing this?**

At my presentations we discuss what is an acceptable range of hurt, a range that is painful but not permanently damaging. Children express what they see as an acceptable range of hurt: someone not inviting you to a party, someone making fun of your silly mistake or sports mess-up, someone rejecting you for a date, or someone ragging on you for not making a team. Some of these things are unkind, but unfortunately they are a normal part of growing up. Once we have established what a normal range is, I ask whether anyone has been or knows a classmate who has been hurt beyond this normal range of scrapes, in ways that unfortunately become gashes. They maim someone and they do not just hurt for a minute. This is the difference between a scrape or a cut and a broken bone—something that is not momentary but that will scar. I explain that no one gets to go through life without getting their feelings hurt, but technology and social media have created yet another avenue to beware of. This avenue sometimes creates a place where it is easier to hurt someone outside the normal range. Children get their feelings hurt, and part of growing up is to learn to deal with that constructively, but this is a different kind of cruelty and a different level of hurt. We want to teach our children that they should not maim their peers.

After we discuss the concept of the normal range of hurt, I ask students whether they or someone they know has been hurt beyond that normal range via social media. At one school I presented at, a student told me about a list that had circulated on social media around the school. It was called the "fugly couples list," in which children had paired their classmates into couples and made jokes about how ugly the pair was or how disparate in attractiveness they were—a "pretty" girl paired with an "ugly" boy and vice versa. The targeted children were aware they were being ridiculed, and they were humiliated and angry and hurting beyond the normal range. As young as third grade, in every school I go to, there is hurt going on that is outside of the normal range. This is why I know we have to step in and do a better job at setting limits and have discussions with our children about the pitfalls of social media.

When we think about children and peer acceptance, we may think of pressure to drink and use drugs or of the "Just Say No" campaigns. But it is difficult to "just say no" to something that surrounds you as completely as technology and social media surround our children. Our children are so steeped in the technology of our culture that it may be less that they are being pressured into using social media in harmful ways, and more that it simply does not occur to them to behave in any other way. Teaching our children to be responsible and mindful about their technology and social media use may involve making them aware of what they are doing as well as why they are doing it. The ability to observe themselves is a wonderful skill to instill, and self-awareness can lead to positive reform.

We Are Not the Same

WE ALL HAVE our own strengths and weaknesses, our own desires and foibles specific to us. We do not all share the same goals, have the same fears, or like the same foods. This is because we are individuals. I know that I have things that others do not and lack things others have. Knowing our strengths is important, and I do not know why we choose to hide that from our children. I realize that our children need to pass their AP, IB, or state exams. We want them to do their personal best. But why do we force endless math tutors on children who are naturally good writers instead of celebrating and embracing the talents they naturally possess? It is important to help our children as early as possible to recognize their own goals and to fulfill the goals that are right for them.

It is human nature to want the thing that everyone else has. I remember wanting my Sassoon Jeans or Calvin Kleins so badly as a teenager, and I was absolutely thrilled when I got them. When my daughter first told me she wanted Uggs for Christmas, I thought, "A hundred and twenty dollars for the ugliest shoe on the planet?" Needless to say, Santa brought Uggs for my daughter. As adults we have had time to form our own opinions about what we like and what we purchase. We purchase certain things because we love the way they look or feel or the way they work, hopefully not just because of their logos. This is our goal as parents: to help our children have solid self-esteem and sense of what is right for them. We all like nice things, but whether those things are glittery or plain or functional or frivolous, should be something we all figure out for ourselves.

It's Not a Secret

IT SHOULD NOT be a secret to our children that self-pride is a goal, and learning to fight the need to overly rely on others' feedback is a skill that we must all work on, at all stages of life. Self-esteem comes from within: it is never gained by other people's approval. Each parent may have a different set of goals for their children, placing more importance on one thing than another. Though most of us want our children to be well-rounded, some parents value academics above all else, while some place the highest importance on sports or on music. If a parent wants to encourage a child to get a 4.0 GPA, be a professional tuba player, or obtain a basketball scholarship, that is up to them. However, all of us need to keep sight of the fact that the end result of our parenting efforts is a person.

Teaching self-worth and self-pride should not be a sneaky endeavor, like hiding the broccoli underneath the mashed potatoes for a picky eater. We are trying to build good, solid people and our children should know that.

One of the most important skills I learned as a teacher is to always let your students know where they are going. I do not walk into a classroom and just start talking, I tell them first what we are going to learn, and how, and why.

When I was teaching second grade, children came into my class knowing how to add and subtract single-digit numbers, small enough problems that they could count the answers on their fingers should they need to. At the beginning of the class, I would tell them, "Now we need to learn to add and subtract numbers larger than ten. We will be able to solve something like this," and I would write on the board "235 + 127." "By the end of the year, we will be able to solve problems like this," and I would write on the board "3425.25—1798.43."

For a second grader, learning to borrow and carry numbers in problems with two or more digits is a three-day lesson. It is difficult and can be confusing, but by telling them on the first day where we were headed, they could understand that the lesson had a purpose. I was giving them a sense of accomplishment every time they took a step toward their goals. Because they knew where they were going, each small step toward that goal made them feel proud and accomplished, knowing that they were doing higher-level work. As we began working with four-digit numbers and decimals, I would tell them, "This is what your parents do in their checkbooks. This is grown-up stuff!" My second graders came in at the beginning of the year counting on their fingers, and by the end of the year they knew all the math they needed to balance a checkbook. That is a fantastic accomplishment, and they had the self-satisfaction of knowing it. Teenagers also have goals. They are in an awkward, difficult place, but they do have goals. Instead of just telling them, "do this" and "do that," when we talk to them in terms of what will help or hinder them in pursuit of those personal goals, they will listen. When we talk to our kids, we need to let them know where they are going. It is not a secret. We want them to be wary of falling prey to peer pressure and to know the likely outcome when and if they do. Once again, we need to let the cat out of the bag and say, **Your goals are important. Let's find ways to help you reach them**.

We can tell children that right now, they are in the process of creating the people they want to be, and getting caught up in reliance on the opinions of their peers will only muddy the waters as they try to find their way. When I worked with second graders on research projects, I did not just tell them to come up with an outline and tell them the steps they needed to take; I told them what the end product needed to be, and we all worked together to figure out the process. Giving guidance will help them figure out their own paths. Self-esteem and pride cannot be based on the approval of their peers but rather on further strengthening their own resolve.

Of course, talking to teens about how they feel is one of the hardest things about being a parent. Having a teenager can be like walking through a minefield. You step one way, then another, and the land is always shifting. What works one day can explode in your face the next. I think the best thing to do is to share the secret: we want our children to feel good about who they are, and we know they want that too. That is the nonnegotiable point. They may not want us nagging them about studying for the SATs or practicing their musical instruments, but they do want to feel good about themselves. I believe that is how we must frame these conversations, about social media as well as about other aspects of life: if this is not making you feel good about yourself, how can we adjust it so you are feeling good about yourself?

I notice parental pressure so strongly in sports. Parents come to watch games, take their children home, and say to them, "If you had just done that one thing differently . . ." Even if we are not overbearing, that kind of constant pressure will kill our children's joy in the sport. Speaking to a friend of mine, I confessed that I had a hard time when my son decided to play baseball. I had played softball throughout my childhood, and it was painful for me to watch him learn, knowing there were tips I could give him that would ultimately make him a better player. I see parents going crazy in the stands, shouting instructions to their children, and I do not want to be that parent!

My friend told me she had read somewhere that a good thing to say to your kids in regard to being a spectator is simply, "I love watching you play." Then leave everything else up to the coaches.

The next time I went to a game, that is what I said to my child afterward. This has shaped my approach to how I talk to my children about their accomplishments. Even after a loss, or a game where my child made mistakes, I tell them, "I love watching you play." If they say, "But I was awful," I just say again, "I don't care; I still love watching you play." It takes the pressure off and allows for personal growth and self-reflection.

We can tell our kids something like, "I love to see how happy you are when you get a good grade," or "I love when you post something you are proud of and don't care about what people say or how many 'likes' you got."

Telling our children *I love watching you play* is not saying *I love when you hit a home run*. It is saying, *I love seeing you happy, I love seeing you fulfilled.* When we cease to be vested in our children winning and focus on what makes them feel good about themselves, we allow them to figure out who they want to be and how to get there. This teaches them to own their successes and failures.

We all want our children to be happy, fulfilled, and confident in themselves. This should not be a secret! If we let our children know that this is their goal, we can help them to internalize it. We can help them to ask, **What do I like? Who am I? What makes me happy? What makes me fulfilled?**

There is no Bible for parenting, and nothing is foolproof. Even the most supportive, thoughtful parents will have a child who drinks, perhaps takes drugs, or posts something they regret on the Internet for the world to see. But my hope is that they will be able to reflect on those actions and ask themselves, **Why did I do that? How did that make me feel?** My character, who I am, matters deeply to me, and I want my children to feel the same way. I sometimes hear the exhortations to "be available" to my children and think, *How much more available can I be?* But being available does not mean jumping to lecture every time a child comes to us; it does not mean forcing conversations on them. It does, I believe, mean letting our children know where they are headed and helping them to create a path that will get them there.

The Allure of the "Like" Button

REGARDLESS OF THE site, one of the traits of social media is the ubiquitous "like" button. A child posts, and friends comment and "like" their post or photo.

During my presentations I ask students, "What is the goal of the 'like' button?" At each and every presentation it is the same answer: to get as many "likes" as possible. I see it as a hamster wheel of validation seeking. Children post seeking a response from their peers. If they get no response the wheel turns slower, and they strive harder to speed it up, posting more and more, hoping to get a reaction. If they receive praise, the wheel speeds up, and they run faster, trying to hold on to that good feeling and chase ever more praise and affirmation. This generation of children grew up with a great deal of affirmation, being praised for their efforts, their participation, and their successes. But while support is important, it is a trait of maturity to understand that we will not always receive affirmation from outside sources, even when we deserve it. It is our job to help our children develop the inner resources to affirm their own accomplishments. As a teacher, I often praise my students both publicly and privately. The public "You did a great job" or "Nice work" always makes a student light up. However, I can tell you that the act of calling a student over privately, pointing out his or her accomplishment, and asking them how that achievement makes them feel makes the child walk, talk, and act in a positive, proud manner, like they are holding a secret that they are proud of. This helps children internalize the feeling of self-confidence and pride. We need to teach today's kids to look inward more often and get in touch with those moments of self-pride. Unfortunately, social media often work against us. Teaching today's child to beware of that "hamster wheel of affirmation" and fight the external need for validation is no easy task, but it will greatly benefit them in the long run. Learning what that internal sense of pride feels like will lead to internal fulfillment.

The "like" is an aspect of social media communication that I see as addictive—there is an instant emotional reward to seeing immediate, positive reinforcement of whatever you have just done. It is like the story of Pavlov, the scientist who trained his dog by ringing a bell right before feeding it. Soon, the dog began to salivate at the sound of the bell, even if there was no food in sight. Reacting to the "like" is similar—we respond to its appearance, even if there is no meaningful content. Similarly, "liking" someone else's post, photo, or video feels like a way of supporting them and of participating in a community, although you have expended only a minimal effort. "Liking" something that all your friends like is a way of saying "I am part of the group" and of saying it publicly.

I know that, for myself, social media can be addictive to a surprising degree. Before I began the Don't Press Send Campaign, I did not even have a Facebook page. I even had to have my niece, Caitlin, set up a Facebook page for me, so I could start one for the sake of promoting the campaign— and now I find myself as easily sucked into it as anyone else. Reading the pages of my friends and acquaintances keeps me involved in the lives of people with whom I am no longer connected. Why? The "like" phenomenon is similar to receiving gold stars in kindergarten: a shiny, simple way of saying, "I recognize you." But we need to ask ourselves and our children, what are we "liking" and why? Are we perpetuating the hamster wheel? Are we Pavlov's dog?

The difficulty of the "like" is that it is such a small thing; it takes no effort to give one, which means that it can feel like no big deal for a child to "like" something that is more unkind than he or she would write on their own. But of course a "like" of an unkind comment can be just as harmful as the comment itself. Multiple "likes" of something hurtful can make the targeted child feel like everyone he or she knows is attacking en masse. Conversely, "liking" things on a friend's page can make us feel like we are connected to them, but in reality that connection, if based on nothing but mutual "likes," is a shallow one. The "like" button has both more and less of an impact than we imagine.

The "like" button is also inherently reactive. A child sees something and clicks it and moves on without much thought. The "like" button encourages exactly the opposite of mindful behavior. Like gamblers at a slot machine, children will keep pushing the button, hoping for a payout that may or may not ever come, not caring if someone gets hurt. Just as the detachment created by the screen means that children are more likely to write things they would never say in person, the "like" button removes still more responsibility from the person who clicks it. After all, they didn't say it themselves. We need to guide our children to recognize that clicking "like" is an active choice and to stop and think before they do it. We can help our children consider what it means to "like," and encourage them to think, **Am I supporting an unkind post? Am I liking something that could hurt someone's feelings?**

Natural Moments of Pride

IT IS NATURAL and healthy to want to share our accomplishments and moments of pride with the people we care about—it is even natural to want the whole world to know about them! But when children start measuring their worth by the reactions of their peers on social media, those natural moments of pride are diminished. For a child who works for years to prepare for an important violin concert or who gets into the college of his or her choice, seeing their announcement or video ignored in favor of photos of someone's new sneakers can be crushing. Worse, it may taint their own pride in their accomplishment. During the course of my presentations, I have heard from young people who found that their excitement in their proudest moments was dampened when they got few "likes" or comments on their posts.

A parent told me about her son, who had been running track since he was eight years old. He had been competing for years, and in high school he finally set a statewide record and was awarded a prestigious scholarship. He excitedly posted about the accomplishment online. The next day, she saw him moping around the house and asked him what was wrong. The boy said, "I only got ten likes."

Pride is internal. Externalizing everything as our children have learned to do, making everything in their lives public, makes them all too dependent on what that public thinks. Children who build their self-images on what people say about them and are constantly on display leave themselves vulnerable. **Pride and self-respect have to come from within, or they will not come at all.** Eventually, children need to learn to chase what makes them proud, not what gets them accolades from their peers. As parents, we need to reinforce this, but social media have made that task much harder.

In part, this comes back to teaching our children to choose privacy. We need to guide them to keep their circles small and limited to those who will truly care about their triumphs and struggles. Their family and their close friends are the people who should and do care when they achieve something great and who will most likely encourage future success. Their social media acquaintances may simply not be as invested in their lives, and that is all right: not everyone should be invested at that level in one another. We need to help our children think carefully about whose opinions they truly respect and whose support they truly value and to focus on the quality of their connections instead of the number of connections.

I tell my students and my own children that when they post online, they need to realize that they are setting themselves up for judgment. Putting something out there means that the reactions they receive are out of their control, and they might not get what they want. I teach my students that if they get a negative comment or if they are ignored, they need to realize that they chose to solicit those responses, positive or negative. We all need to learn to develop thick skins, to build our inner resources so that we can withstand the negative feedback we will all sometimes receive. But we can also choose what we open ourselves up to. In addition, it is important for children to understand that what people pay attention to online does not reflect what actually matters. There is no telling what will grab the attention of the public. Advertisers spend billions of dollars to try to predict that, and they frequently fail. Just as we must teach our children that a person's glamorous online profile does not reflect the full reality of that person's life, we must help them see that what people do and do not "like" depends on a whole host of uncontrollable factors.

For example, when a child posts something online, their friends may or may not even see it. Their friends may look at the site at home, half paying attention while doing their homework. They may be reading on their phone while riding a bus or chatting with three people at once while scanning the site. They may look at it during their lunch period or at 3:00 a.m. Site algorithms may not show them the post at all if they do not seek it out. Some friends may see a post and choose not respond for their own reasons—if a child posts about getting into the college of his or her choice, for example, friends may not "like" it because they did not get in and are jealous, or because they are so preoccupied with their own college search that any mention of someone else's success makes them anxious. On social media as in life offline, how people react to us often has far more to do with them than with us.

Social media moves quickly; people interact with it in different ways, and our children need to learn that there is little to be inferred by who does or does not "like" their posts. I have told my students if they want to post something and they feel confident that they will not be constantly checking and rechecking to see the comments, then go ahead. But I also teach them to ask, **Am I posting looking for a response or do I just want to share it?** Most children will admit that they are just looking for praise and affirmation. We need to teach our children to be honest with themselves. If they are going to feel bad if they do not get the response they want, they need to rethink posting at all, because otherwise they are just jumping back on that hamster wheel. This encourages a desperate feeling.

One-Upping Each Other

BECAUSE THE GOAL of our children is to get a large number of "likes," that goal has quickly turned into a game of one-upmanship. I have heard a number of stories in which the pursuit of "likes" has gotten children into serious danger. One story in particular sticks in my head, illustrating for me the serious outcomes that can occur when the "like" button becomes a competition.

Two friends were driving in a car, and when they passed a 45 MPH speed limit sign, the passenger took a picture of it and posted it to Instagram. Then he took a picture of the car's speedometer, which read "55 MPH." The pictures got a large number of "likes," and one response: "Beat that tomorrow night. I will double your 'likes.'" As you may already have guessed, another group of children did the same thing at 65 MPH. I do not know the outcome of this case, but we can all imagine what could have happened. As a parent, I am sure that reading this you feel sick, because children have always tried to compete and one-up each other. However, social media add another layer of complication, because they don't even have to be present to pressure one another. In the course of my presentations I have heard a number of disturbing stories in which the pursuit of the "likes" online got children into serious offline danger. Many children find themselves pushed to do things they would otherwise not try when their peers "egg" them on.

When how much you are appreciated is literally quantifiable, it can be hard to avoid games of one-upmanship. A child might think, *If my friend got 100 "likes" with his stunt, I'll do a crazier stunt and get 200!* Social capital is often subtle and difficult to measure; we do not always accurately perceive how well we are liked or how much we are respected. But the "like" button can send the message, "You are exactly this popular." It is not an accurate message—what people "like" often has to do with what moment they happen to be in online, what happens to catch their eye, and what else they are in the middle of doing. But the idea of having a number that tells you how socially successful you are is enticing, and it is easy to see why our children play the numbers game and try to do everything they can to bring that number higher.

In person, we see this kind of thing as well—large groups of teenagers are not well-regarded for their decision-making skills—but online, the group of people commenting and pressuring can be much, much larger. That group of 500 friends may not be made up of people a child would take orders from one-on-one, but if half of them comment on a stunt or video, it can feel like a crowd mandate. Many children report being pushed to do things like drink to excess at parties—being encouraged to "do a shot for me" from someone who is not present, or posting pictures of themselves drinking, getting "likes," and drinking more to get more "likes." Chasing the "like" becomes a destructive cycle.

There is also the question of what message is being sent with that click of the "like" button. When children "like" one another's self-destructive or risky behaviors, they are pushing one another to be daredevils, to one-up each other and impress their peers. But there is a darker edge to that—if a child posting about getting drunk at a party or performing dangerous stunts gets lots of "likes," they are being encouraged to self-destruct. Many of us have known—or been—children who act out because of depression, confusion, difficulties at home, or even abuse. A child who is engaging in harmful activities out of distress and sees his or her peers "liking" those antics may feel that their pain is being deliberately ignored and their self-harm encouraged, leading them to greater depths of self-destruction. We need to encourage our children to think about what they are pushing their friends to do and whether they themselves are being pushed. A "like" is often just the thoughtless click of a button, and our children need to learn to recognize it as such, once again reinforcing the importance of that mindful pause and reiterating the difference between a reaction and a response. In addition, we need to teach our children not to overvalue how many "likes" they receive.

As the administrator of the Don't Press Send Campaign's Facebook page, I can see not only how many people "like" a posting, but also how many people viewed it. I know that when I see 106 views and only 4 likes, I feel an inevitable disappointment. *I wonder why this did not get the same attention as other posts,* I think. *This is a lot of work; I hope it is not all being done in vain.* I worry: *Am I making a big enough impact?* It is discouraging to see such a small response. But having experienced disappointment throughout my life has fostered my ability as an adult to push past it. As a longtime educator, I know to tell myself, *If I help 100 people, great. If I help four people, great. As long as I am educating.* I have trained myself to post and not look back, to remind myself that anything done with good intent will create good in the world. I am an adult, and this is hard for me, and I know it must be that much harder for young people. It is human nature to want feedback, to know if you have done a good job at work, but we cannot always expect to receive it.

One thing we can do is provide feedback for those around us. I love going to restaurants and telling the manager how good our service was; usually managers hear only complaints. My son has never been a big reader and rarely reads except for his schoolwork. Recently, however, he found a series by a new author, and he has sped through four of her books in three months, and so I wrote to the author to tell her, "You have done this for my son—you have captured his attention." We all want positive feedback; we all want the rush the "like" button provides by showing us someone's approval. But we can get it, and give it, at a more personal, thoughtful level. By making someone aware of the good they have done in the world, we can spread that positive spirit. I am a firm believer that a person who is appreciated will always do more than expected.

External Validation

MANY CHILDREN HAVE become accustomed to oversharing online, as we have all witnessed in dreaded posts: from a cake they made, to a house without parents, to how they're feeling, who they are upset with, and where they are going to be. They are looking for a reaction. In a previous chapter I discussed the phenomenon of taking pictures and videos of events while never being mindfully present for the event. This kind of attitude makes life into a public performance, with an audience that includes everyone whose friend request you have ever accepted. When our children put everything they do, think, and feel out there for the world to see, it is no wonder that they take "likes" and comments to heart. Externalizing everything means going outside the self for validation; by sharing everything online, they are seeking approval from everyone but themselves. They are playing to an audience, and not always a generous one.

It can be difficult to watch this, but perhaps we can help our children to realize that "likes" are not a true measure of one's self or one's accomplishments, and looking to one-up each other will only end in disappointment or hurt. Most of us want our children to find their validation internally and to surround themselves with people who truly support and care for them. In practice, they will always seek out peer approval, as we do ourselves, but perhaps we can help them to be more selective about whom they choose as their audience.

Some performers imagine their ideal viewer when they perform, some writers imagine a particular person reading their work—both tailor their work to the audience they most want to please. We can encourage our children to do the same, then act on it. We can help them strive to think about whom they want in their audience, whose opinions and support they truly want to have—and then learn to focus only on the people whose response they truly value. My target audience for this book is thoughtful and reflective parents and educators who want to work together toward a kind, careful, and positive cyber community for our children.

A good example of a positive outcome is when internal pride wins over the need for external validation. When a friend's daughter won a science scholar award, I came across it in a local paper and never saw it mentioned on social media or by her parents, with whom I have a close relationship. I gave the girl my congratulations when I next saw her, and she said, "thank you" with a glow of pride. It was clear that she was so proud of herself that she did not need to tell the world; it was enough to know she had succeeded. I think that is what we all should aim for.

One question we might help our children to examine is, what does a "like" mean? Though we cannot completely divorce ourselves from the opinions of others, we can think about which opinions should hold weight. A "like" is in itself a shallow comment. It is generic and takes almost no effort on the part of the giver.

Thirteen-year-old Huan might feel bad about himself when he does not get enough "likes" on his posts. One response to this might be to dismiss his need for "likes" as shallow, but his parents might also try asking him what those "likes" mean to him: What does he want his friends to think when they see that post? What does he want people to feel about him? **What would a like mean?** His parents can ask him how he feels about himself. Would he be proud of a friend who accomplished the same thing? Does he feel proud of himself?

Parents can encourage our children not to simply hit the "like" button but to think, **What do I "like" about this post?** Is it funny? Am I impressed by the accomplishment? Do I wish I could do that, too? I tell my students, if you "like" something, back it up with a positive comment: "That is so funny!"; "Congratulations!"; "Great photo!" If you cannot think of a kind, positive comment, then maybe you shouldn't be posting anything. Learning to praise other people's accomplishments is a good thing. I know adults who are unable to praise the impressive work or good fortune of others, but it is important for us all to remember that we are never diminished by someone else's accomplishment. Even if we are envious, it feels better to reach down deep and try to feel genuinely happy for them than to be bitter. Pushing ourselves to be positive is good for us, and striving to be more specific than a simple "like" makes us better friends. We can urge our children to think of a real comment every time they want to hit "like." **Instead of simply clicking "like," post a positive comment!** Or better yet, wait and tell your friend what you think in person.

Mindful Affirmation

THE POWER OF the "like" button is a human Pavlov's dog experiment; even if there is no food, the dog will still salivate over the sound of the bell. We need to guide our children to stop and think, even before they do something as seemingly inconsequential as clicking "like." Just as we must teach them never to type something they would not say face-to-face, we must teach them not to "like" anything they would not say themselves. Being mindful of our impact on the world means being aware that even the smallest of our choices can have significant effects on the people around us. Part of growing up is to look around us and consider the things we do by habit and to question the norms we have accepted. That is what the Don't Press Send Campaign seeks to do: we need to reevaluate what is a social norm, what is acceptable, and what is healthy. We need to teach our children to look at what "everybody" is doing, and ask themselves *why* everybody is doing it. We can teach them to stop and be mindful before they hit the "like" button and ask themselves:

- » **Do I want to get on that "hamster wheel"?**
- » **Do I really support this?**
- » **Would I encourage my friend to do this if he or she were standing in front of me?**

When they are on the other side of this, getting, or hoping for "likes," we can encourage them to consider what a "like" really means, and to ask:

- » **Why am I posting this?**
- » **Will I be upset if I share this accomplishment and get only a few likes?**
- » **Do I truly value this person's opinion?**
- » **Who do I want in my audience?**

CHAPTER SIX
Mindful Healthy Habits

» What is a healthy habit?

A **healthy habit** is a behavior that is beneficial to your physical or mental health.

ON A RECENT trip to Mexico with my family, my son expressed interest in visiting a site of ancient Mayan ruins. Although it was a three-hour bus ride out of our way and I would have been much happier sitting on the beach, I took him to see them. Along the way, my children were all entertaining themselves with their electronics, playing games on their phones to pass the time. As we drove, we drove through some areas of obvious and extreme poverty, where the streets, the houses, and the people showed clear evidence of need. I had to bring the surroundings to their attention by taking their electronics/technology away from them. We saw dogs so thin that their ribs were visible.

We saw homes that had no windows, with very little furniture. We saw adults with unkempt clothing on, who had no teeth, and there were broken-down cars and abandoned buildings. There were neighbors gathered together talking and eating and laughter being shared. Although my children do not live a sheltered life and have seen and experienced hardship, this was poverty at a level they had never witnessed before. It was a far cry from the beautiful resort we had just left an hour ago.

"It makes me feel sad to look at this," one of my children said. "Can I please have my phone back?" My response was, "That's good. Feeling for others is a good thing." I realized that not only do we miss out on our surroundings and life lessons, we have learned to use our technological devices as an avoidance tactic.

The screen is not only a way of detaching from the effects our actions have on others; it is a way of detaching from the whole world around us. Video games may keep our children entertained, but they also keep them from seeing, and empathizing with, the sometimes harsh circumstances of the people who surround them. It was painful for my children to see the way much of the world lives, but some things are meant to be painful, and blocking them out does not make them cease to exist.

Creating healthy habits regarding our use of technology does not start or stop with those devices; it is about learning to live as healthier people and create a healthier world.

Learning Mindfulness

MINDFULNESS IS SIMPLY the art of **paying attention on purpose**. I came to the practice of mindfulness through my son. When he was struggling with his attention deficit hyperactivity disorder, we sent him to see Dr. Jolie Silva, with New York Behavioral Health. Dr. Silva is a behavioral therapist who specializes in mindfulness. I wanted to understand what my son was going through and was hoping to be able to help him process it and incorporate helpful techniques and routines into our home life. I myself began taking classes through mindfulschools.org to better educate myself as both a parent and a teacher. The fundamentals of mindfulness and curriculum courses have guided me in many ways. Mindfulness has become a daily practice in my life and has changed my perspective on the world and enlightened me to a healthier level. I started this practice to help my son, but in turn, what it gave me was life changing.

Mindfulness, I learned, is about doing one thing at a time and focusing on every aspect of that thing. Everyone can benefit from a little more mindfulness in their life. It lessens distraction and multitasking and increases focus. Mindful techniques are used to help people change their diets or quit smoking; to help people with anxiety, depression, or attention disorders; in trauma therapy and, perhaps most impressively, pain management. One of the first things my mindfulness therapist suggested was that I pick an activity I do multiple times every day, something like washing my hands. She told me to focus, each time I did it, on every aspect of the experience, like the feel of the warm water, the smell of the soap, and the sensation of rubbing my hands together. I chose the simple act of opening locks with a key. For the next week, every time I opened or closed my front door, I took special notice of the way the key slid into the lock, the catch of each little groove, and the resistance as I turned the key.

I found that it worked. Putting all of my attention onto that single small action recalled me to my surroundings from whatever I had been thinking about. It made me aware of what was around me and what I was doing. We spend much of our lives thinking about the next thing, even as we are still doing this thing. Learning mindfulness techniques helped me to concentrate on what is happening right now. Many schools are now incorporating mindful education and there has been an increased awareness of mindfulness. Maybe you have been hearing the word more and more often, hence the title of this book. The term is catching on, even becoming a catchphrase, and I believe that is because its importance is catching on. I am happy to hear that schools are adapting this practice in educating our children. Incorporating mindfulness is an educational gift that keeps on giving and will help in every aspect of their lives. I applaud these schools' innovative and holistic approach to educating all parts of the child. Social and emotional development is just as important as math and science. If you are interested in learning more, go to mindfulschools.org.

Setting a Mindful Example

WE ARE SETTING a non-mindful example for our children when they are very young, and I worry about a generation of toddlers who constantly see everyone around them glued to their phones. When a just-barely-verbal child is bouncing out of his stroller seat, pointing and yelling, "Dog! Dog! Dog!" at an animal he has never named before, and his parent is distracted by the phone, that parent is missing a major moment in their child's development. Moreover, the child's discovery is not being reinforced. The parent is not saying, "Yes, that is a dog! Isn't it fluffy? What kind of dog do you think that was?" and perhaps later at home, "Tell your mother and brother what we saw at the park today!" This kind of dialogue fosters exploration, curiosity, and language development, and we want to encourage that, not ignore it. I would give anything for a few moments back with my toddlers. Those years are so full of discovery, and yet they are so fleeting.

I understand the impulse to give a small child a phone or tablet to play with while you are in the grocery store, as it must make the process of shopping infinitely faster and easier than wrangling a toddler up and down the aisles. When I think to when my children were that age, I can imagine moments when that kind of distraction would have made my life considerably easier. I raised my children during the Baby Mozart era. I would put on that CD to entertain my child, just so I could take a shower. I recall many hectic days—especially with my twins—when I played the video over and over, just so we could make it through the day. But I would feel badly if I overused it, treating it like a babysitter, because nothing beats human interaction. There is so much available to parents today to distract children and keep them busy that we need to be careful of overuse.

The parent who constantly uses technology to distract their child is also missing out on a lot. I remember all the great moments of discovery that happened while buying groceries: my son learning for the first time what the names of brightly colored vegetables were, or my daughter seeing her favorite cartoon character in a life-sized cardboard cutout. I recall showing my oldest son tomatoes and smiling as he came to understand that the tomatoes growing on the vine in our backyard were the same thing as the tomatoes being sold in this store and that both were used to make tomato sauce. At that age, everything is new, and everything is an adventure. Places that are mundane to us are brand-new worlds to them. Giving them an addictive toy like a tablet robs them of those discoveries and robs us of the joy of watching them explore. It is truly amazing to watch everything in their little world amaze them, to see the lights go on in their eyes, to see their excitement, because every single thing is new, and they are constantly making connections. It helped me learn to value things, because they appreciated the little things. As parents, it forces us to slow down and say, "Wow, look at the beauty they see in all the things around them." Children teach us, too, and one of the things they can truly teach us is mindfulness.

When we are tied to those devices, we are setting the example for them to do the same, but we are also sending a message about what we value. When we are constantly attached to our phones, ignoring our children as they reach out for attention, we are communicating that we value those devices more than we value those relationships. When we miss our child's first sight of something majestic, like a bluebird, or a dump truck, we are communicating that the phone is more important than they are. This is not to say that parents should be constantly available, but that when we are with our children, we should be fully present.

I believe that our cultural addiction to technology is part of a larger picture. We are constantly pulled in different directions, and I see my friends and neighbors constantly multitasking. We are keeping up with our own lives—our work responsibilities, our homes, and our families—but we are also preoccupied with managing the lives of our children. We drive them to and from school instead of letting them walk or take the bus; we schedule sports, music lessons, classes, and volunteer activities for them every day, clean three different uniforms, and help them do their homework and practice their instruments.

Once, the image of the mother who scheduled her toddler's day to the minute was a symbol of overachievement, but now scheduling our children for constant activities, and making sure they get there, has become the norm. We are not doing it because we expect too much of our children, and would do so regardless of the culture. We are doing it because it has become the baseline for how to raise children in certain parts of the world. We feel that if we fail to juggle multiple activities, sometimes for numerous children, we will be failing them, leaving them unable to compete for college and the job market with children whose mothers didn't refuse to buy them designer sports socks.

As a culture we have come to value people who are constantly busy. Being connected to the workplace at all hours of the day is frequently expected. The adults we see checking email at 9:00 p.m. on a night out at the theater may not simply be trying to look important; they may be doing it because they fear that if they do not, they will look disengaged and unambitious, as though they do not care about their work. Being busy all of the time is a way of showing that we are keeping up, that we are worth something to a culture that values productivity above all else. Technology has evolved to allow us to be constantly available, and now many of us feel that we must be.

I see my peers working hard to maintain the Supermom image, rushing around taking their children from one thing to another, while maintaining their own life responsibilities. When we are constantly struggling to multitask, when do we ever model downtime or unstructured time? When do we allow ourselves or our children to focus on one thing, to become absorbed in learning about something that intrigues them without a deadline or grade attached to it? When do we let them play in the mud, with no purpose other than to get dirty? When I was a child, I remember getting in trouble for laughing—I would laugh so much and so hard I annoyed everyone around me. That kind of intense laughter was a beautiful part of my childhood, but I rarely see that kind of laughter among children today. I rarely see them let loose with that kind of abandon. They are as focused as their parents on keeping up with the demands of the age.

I try to tell my children, and my students, "I am the grown up—I hold the big suitcase, you hold the carry-on." What I mean is that the big worries are mine: how to pay the mortgage so we have a place to live, whether they are being prepared for the life ahead of them, for college, for a job, or whether they are learning healthy habits and communications skills. But right now, I see kids carrying the big suitcases, and they are not strong enough for that. We want them to build up to that, and take it on when they are older. In their kid-sized carry-ons should be age-appropriate responsibility: their books, their homework, their activities, their chores, doing their best, having fun. The little suitcase should only carry the essentials, their responsibilities for the here and now. That suitcase only fits what they need right now. We, the adults, need to prepare them for the future and give them opportunities to grow, but those anxieties belong in the big suitcase, and we need to be the ones to carry it.

Having written my graduate thesis on the power of play, I clearly see the importance of allowing children to learn through exploration. The value of play in social interaction as a learning medium has been well documented by renowned theorists such as Jean Piaget and Maria Montessori. Their research supports the belief that interactive play and discovery are crucial to learning. Children learn numerous skills through play, such as negotiating, sharing, compassion, risk-taking, and empathy. All of those skills lead to effective communication and successful personal relationships as well as leadership abilities and good citizenship. These are the skills that help us to live and work with others and to enjoy and appreciate our lives. Behavior in early childhood predicts future success, and we need to foster these skills at the early childhood level.

I strongly believe that we have it backward. Building a strong child from the get-go is vital, and building life skills that will foster academic success cannot go by the wayside. I believe that our children's reliance on technology is weakening their social and emotional life skills, and putting so much emphasis on test scores is only making things worse. Until parents start realizing that we are sacrificing our kids' social and emotional growth for the sake of a grade on a test, this will not get better. Just like kids walk and talk when they are ready, they will read when they are ready; you cannot force reading on a four-year-old who is not ready for it. Making children take tests for which they are not ready destroys their emotional competency.

Something that we all need to accept is that no matter where you live, there will always be a bell curve with a top, middle, and bottom. Not everyone's child can be a genius, and that is okay. Preparing children for success means guiding them to do their own personal best and teaching them to accept themselves for who they are.

We have to begin to look at self-development and self-acceptance as being an important part of overall health. It is about our mental and emotional health, and our children learn from our example. If we are constantly doing six things at once, so will they. If they see us texting while they tell us a story, they will do the same to their friends. If we are constantly rushing from one thing to another, without a pause for breath, we are teaching them to live a frenetic, stressful lifestyle. If we insist that everything they do be geared toward increasing their college marketability, how will they learn to find joy or their true passions? One of my pet peeves about scholastics and activities is the way in which the community service aspect is presented. As a child, I learned to bring in my neighbor's garbage pail even when no one was looking, because it was the right thing to do. It was not a question of appearances but of pride and being part of a community. Today, while it is a good thing for schools and organizations that work with young people to encourage service hours, the way the go about it, with required hours and lots of social media self-congratulation, is beside the point.

It is lovely to see a group of neighborhood children mowing lawns for people who cannot, but when I see their parents posting pictures of their children doing it, with captions like, "Oh, what great kids," the meaning of the act changes. The motivation is not internal, it is to boast. Outside praise does not become internal pride, and only internal pride feeds happiness and self-esteem.

I live on Long Island, which was hit hard by Hurricane Sandy, and a town very close to mine was nearly destroyed. Everyone helped. Young and old, we all pitched in without hesitation, not thinking about clocking hours or getting credit. It was a wonderful thing to see. But then I began to see parents posting incessantly about their children's efforts on social media. When everything our children do is documented and broadcast to the world, it is no wonder they value external praise so highly. We need to notice when we are perpetuating this cycle and pause before we post. You can simply ask them how they felt about what they did. You will hear firsthand the internal pride they have and you can leave it at that. It is then that they will begin to feel that pride and want to feed it. Posting about these accomplishments could actually be taking their inner sense of pride away.

We all agree this generation grew up with a lot of praise. Maybe they don't need more. We are teaching them to miss the point, to do good because it will make them feel good inside. I do not think it is wrong for schools to ask their students to perform community service. In the religion class I teach, my students are required to do ten hours of community service as a requirement for Confirmation. But service should not be about filling a certain number of hours or checking a box on a college application—it should come from a true sense of caring about a neighbor or taking pride in a community. Our children need to ask themselves, **Would I be doing this if no one was watching?** It feels good to do the right thing, and when you get accustomed to that feeling, you just do it.

Engaging Mindfully

WHEN USED TO excess, cell phones and tablets are anti-mindfulness devices. They take us out of our surroundings and allow us to completely detach from what is going on around us. This does not mean that the devices themselves are bad; it means that we have an extra challenge—we need to learn how to use them mindfully.

I have discussed, in previous chapters, the idea of having tech-free times. We can encourage our families to leave cell phones outside the bedroom and dock tablets after 9:00 p.m. We can ban tech from dinner and other family activities and make sure we all have alarm clocks separate from our phones. We can also beware not to use them as an avoidance tactic. But we also need to think about how to engage mindfully when we are using them.

Many of us have experienced the "rabbit hole" of the Internet. We open a single page, then follow a link to another and another and another. Whether it is a news site or a social media site, there is always another link to follow. Suddenly hours have passed, and you know exactly what your mother's cousin's best friend's had for dinner, but you still haven't asked your sister for that recipe you wanted. This aspect of the Internet is addictive in nature, but just as we need to teach our children to pause before they post, we can teach them—and ourselves—to think before we even pick up or turn on a device. We can ask questions like, **What am I going to use this for?**

All too often we turn to a phone or computer to fill time, rather than to accomplish a specific task. We spend hours on social media because it is there, reacting to the things other people have posted without a clear goal in mind. Before we turn on the computer or open a browser, it is worth making a plan. We can ask, **Do I need to check my email? Do I need to do research? Do I want to look at social media? How long am I going to use this?**

The Internet may not be infinite, but it surely contains more information than a single person could examine in a lifetime, which means that going online "until I'm done" is an unrealistic goal. Many of us have seen our children, our friends, our spouses, or ourselves go online at some point in the evening and never step away from the computer until it is long past time to go to bed. Before we start, we can stop and ask ourselves, **How much time do I have for this? What else do I want to do today?** Just as if we are on a diet and need to think, How many high-calorie treats am I going to allow myself this week? Cutting back and being healthier does not mean we can never have our favorite treats again (and as many of us have learned the hard way, this is just setting ourselves up for failure). Being healthier about what we eat means having a cookie once in a while, not eating a whole box every day. Tempering our use of technology involves the same thought processes and the same techniques. We can come up with strategies to interrupt our online activities, like setting a timer for an hour after we start or setting a limit on how many social media pages we can look at per day. We can encourage our children to do the same and to "like" only three things per day, so they are limiting the mindless ritual of the "like" button, thinking carefully about where and how they want to spend their time, and remembering that even by reading you are participating.

How Do I Want to Engage?

"HOW DO I want to engage" is a larger, philosophical question, which I have discussed at length throughout this book, but it can also be a practical question. Before going online, we can think about whether we want to be social or if we simply want to read. Planning ahead can keep us from starting interactions we will later regret, and it can keep us focused on doing what we need to do, then stepping away from the device. Social media that let everyone on our friend list know that we are online means that we frequently seem, or even feel, like we must be open to chatting with anyone. It is important for our children to remember that they have a choice. They can always ignore a request to chat or decline politely. Teaching your children to simply say, "Got to run, talk to you soon," gives them a quick exit that will empower your children to realize that they have the control and willpower to walk away. They can talk to people who make them feel uplifted and block people who make them feel down on themselves.

Some things we can help them to consider are:

- » **Do I want to chat with anyone, or comment on posts?**
- » **Who do I want to chat with?**
- » **Do I have something specific that I want to post?**
- » **Do I just want to look, and for how long?**
- » **Am I in the right mood to interact on social media?**
- » **Will this make me feel good?**

Many of us have days when looking at social media just makes us feel bad about ourselves, and our children are even more vulnerable to that than we are. Social media is not a mandatory daily activity, as much as it may sometimes feel like one, and if looking at the glamorous personas other people post of their own lives is going to make a child feel sad or insecure, it is best to realize that before starting, and just not open that door.

Another danger in using technology while not in a positive state of mind is the angry or angst-ridden email fired off in a quick response and sent without reflection. Many of us have sent or received one of these, and it is not a good feeling to be on either side of the interaction. We can help our children learn not to respond in the moment when things online are either being misunderstood or being written with strong emotion. One of the great advantages of the Internet is that it is possible to step back from an email before responding, cool down, and carefully consider an appropriate response. We can encourage our children to take that advantage and ask questions like:

- » **Am I tired? Sad? Angry? Upset?**
- » **Am I in the right frame of mind to engage with anyone?**
- » **Is there a particular response that I am hoping to get from someone?**
- » **Is my response appropriate and proportional?**
- » **Could this be misinterpreted?**
- » **How does using this device in my usual way make me feel?**

Our children need to rethink their social media usage and choose to partake in things that uplift them and make them feel good. Engaging in destructive dialogue is a choice, and it is an option they do not have to make. Many of us have stepped away from the computer screen feeling bleary-eyed and exhausted, even though physically we are just sitting there, staring at words or pictures on a page. This is because inertia is itself exhausting; when we spend too much time doing something that does not enrich us, we do not feel good. We feel better when we engage with the world, when we stretch our brains and learn something new and when we reinforce positive thought patterns. Sometimes we feel good when we give ourselves over to relaxation, but time spent mindlessly on the computer is rarely relaxing. Instead, it is compulsive, unfocused, and mood-altering. We leap from page to page, click endlessly on new links, and constantly change direction. We need to think before we sit down, **How will I feel in an hour if I do this now?**

Doing One Thing at a Time

MINDFULNESS MEANS DOING one thing at a time. When our children go to parties and events and spend their time taking pictures and posting about what they are doing, they are not fully engaging with their surroundings. Mindfulness means being an active participant and learning not to worry about how they will look in photographs later. Photos are a two-dimensional representation of a fleeting moment; their value is that they help us to recall the full memory. Memory is sights and sounds, scents and emotions, and our children will not form the most important parts of their memories if all they are focused on is creating a picture and posting for an audience.

Being an active participant means knowing what is going on around you and deciding how you want to participate. If there is a kickball game going on at a picnic and you don't want to play, don't stand halfheartedly in the outfield while texting—throw yourself into the game and see if you might like it. Or go and find something you do want to do, like helping on the grill, talking to a friend, or being the umpire. When we use technology to unofficially opt out of the things we are unenthusiastic about, we miss out on the chance to find something to do that we can do wholeheartedly.

Missing Out

IT IS EASY to feel like a killjoy when we tell our children to put down their electronics. *"But I was having fun playing this game!"* or *"But I'm in the middle of a group chat!"* they might say. But we might ask them to think, what are you missing out on while you are doing that? We can help them learn to prioritize. No one has time for everything.

One change I have made that has made me feel that I am at least trying to instill better social skills is very simple—when my children have social gatherings I have them and their friends place their cell phones in a bowl in the kitchen. If their parents need to reach them, I have the phones and can answer them, but taking away their technology means that the kids are forced to interact and have fun together, rather than sitting silently or spending all their time looking at videos together (which is, unfortunately, what they often do, and we only see the tops of their heads, not their cute faces).

Surprisingly, I have met with almost no resistance. When my daughter held a surprise party for one of her friends, the guests themselves appointed someone to be on cell phone patrol and collect the devices for my bowl. When they come over they sometimes chant, "Cell phones in the bowl! Cell phones in the bowl!" Not only is this policy acceptable to them, I believe it is often a relief for them to have a break.

I have the same policy in the car. For long trips, I let my children entertain themselves with their devices, but if we are driving around town, they can talk to one another, or to me, for fifteen minutes. I believe that by teaching them that they do not need their phones at every second, I am teaching them necessary coping and social skills for life.

Many children, including mine, are missing essential skills because of their access to and dependence on technology. I know a number of children who have no sense of direction because they have GPS built into their phones and available in their cars. They even program in the address for a place they have been to a hundred times. They never needed to learn how to get there by memory, and so they never did. They are missing out on a deep-seated sense of their surroundings. By remaining constantly glued to their phones in public, they discourage anyone from coming up to them to ask directions or start a conversation. A video I feel illustrates this beautifully, called "Look Up!" can be found on my website at DontPressSend.org.

Though we want our children to be wary of strangers, interacting with the people around them in minor ways is a part of our social fabric. These are some of the things that make us a part of the world. Smiling at passersby creates an atmosphere of kindness; it feels good, encourages them to smile back, and puts a spring in everyone's step. If I catch someone's eye walking down the street I smile at them and they smile back—that is the human connection that we share.

Even those minor interactions have meaning, and I find that I miss them when people are replaced with technology. I particularly dislike the self-checkout at stores. I don't want to go to self-checkout. I don't work there, the store is not paying me to do that labor, and they are not making prices cheaper. They are threatening the jobs of people who need the work. But in my daily life, I want that interaction with the cashier. Many times I have had encounters that changed my perspective, even in small exchange. At CVS recently, I saw a college-aged cashier wearing a college T-shirt. When I asked, he told me his brother went there and loved it. My son is looking at colleges right now and this school could be the perfect fit for my son. I would never have heard of it had I not spoken with the cashier.

I don't want to go to a machine that malfunctions constantly. I want to talk. The people working there have something to offer, and taking a job someone needs and replacing them with a computer is unnecessary and benefits no one. I have been spending much of my time at home, writing my book and putting my program together. I am often alone! This is my human interaction, and people crave this! I have family and friends to interact with at other times than during the work day, but there are many who do not. Many of us have seen elderly or isolated people for whom the highlight of the day is to buy toothpaste and talk to the person at the counter to have a pleasant interaction. There is less office work because of technology, and less human interaction. The flexibility many people find in working from home is great, but societies, and communities, are built on social interaction. It is a basic need, and it cannot be replaced.

On Long Island, most residents know the North Shore from the South Shore and know that Manhattan is west and Montauk is east. My children know those things, but that is all the geography that they know. When my son is going somewhere, he simply puts the coordinates into his GPS. If I ask him about his route, he just says, "I don't know. Don't worry, I'll get there."

I love GPS for myself, but I am also concerned that my son relies on it as his only navigational guide. He does not know what neighborhoods he will be passing through or if it is worth taking a longer route to avoid a dangerous area. In fact, the GPS does not even provide a full map, so you are not looking at what is surrounding the area you are in; you simply follow the route without even looking at where you are going from a wider perspective. What will happen if your car breaks down or your phone dies? Though GPS is an incredibly useful technology, it is worth asking ourselves what skills we are allowing to atrophy when we use it exclusively.

The most irreplaceable thing our children are missing is, quite simply, experience. It is wonderful that screens have given us access to things we might otherwise never see—the Northern Lights, innumerable videos of kittens, live concerts, or political actions happening halfway across the world. But almost by definition, our experiences are always better in person. I recently saw a picture in the news of a man sitting on a boat, staring at his phone—as a humpback whale swam by not three feet away from him (this picture can be found on the DontPressSend.org website under "media"). People wait with hopeful anticipation going on whale watches in harbors where they congregate, and they do it knowing that they may not see a whale at all. This man missed what for many people would be a once-in-a-lifetime experience, because he was absorbed in his phone at the wrong moment.

Ironically, many people feel that they need to constantly be in touch via technology because they do not want to miss out on anything. Whether it is a parent wanting to keep up with work, a child afraid of missing out on who is dating whom, who made what team, where the next party is, or the latest middle school feud, the urge to be constantly connected is born from a feeling that we might be left out of something important. We need to hold on to that feeling, but apply it to the world more immediately around us.

We also need to give ourselves permission to miss things: to miss calls, to miss trends, to miss gossip. We can give our emergency contact information out for true emergencies and let all of the rest go. Those of us who are not in lifesaving professions can generally let something go without anyone dying. (Those who are in lifesaving professions, by all means, keep your devices on!) We may need to sacrifice one kind of connectedness, but the richer, more valuable kind of connection is the one that comes from accepting that doing one thing mindfully means letting everything else go for a while. This means attending to what is physically right in front of you at every given moment. If you're on the phone, talk. If you're typing, type. If you're watching a movie, enjoy the movie. Learn to be fully engaged in whatever it is you are doing.

Empathy

EMPATHY IS THE mindful awareness of someone else's feelings. We begin to teach it to our children when they are scarcely old enough to talk. "How would it make you feel if your sister hit you?" we say, and hope for a look of shame that indicates our child is able to put him- or herself in someone else's shoes and see things from their perspective. We sometimes talk about empathy as an inborn trait, and to an extent it may be, but really, it is something we learn. Empathy is situational. We have it more for people we care about than people we do not know and less for people whom we consider reprehensible than for people we admire. Empathy is something we teach, and as such, it is a skill that our children can strengthen with practice. If you have not seen CNN's program *#Being13* I highly recommend viewing it for an eye-opening and clear portrayal of the need for empathy. Not only does it give a clear landscape of the mind of a thirteen-year-old and why they feel the need to be so involved in social media, it clearly shows that the screen has disconnected our children and their empathetic skills need to be strengthened. You can watch and stream it on the Don't Press Send website at DontPressSend.org

I have discussed the detachment of the screen, but once we become aware of it, that detachment becomes a choice. Children can choose to allow themselves that detachment or to fight against it by being mindful when they are using social media, asking, **Am I considering how the other person feels?**

Moreover, when used deliberately, social media can actually help us to build our empathy skills, if we choose to do so. One of the greatest strengths of the Internet is that we can read about and even talk with people from dramatically different circumstances than our own. When we read something that makes us feel unknowledgeable, we can ask the person about it, or we can do research on the topic until we understand it. Part of pausing before we post is realizing that we need to pay closer attention to the here and now.

As parents, most of us think carefully and constantly about how to raise our children with good values, how to give them a reliable moral compass that will remain with them even when we are absent, and how to encourage them to do the right thing, even when no one is watching. We teach them empathy, and we need to teach them to trust their gut feeling—to feel, viscerally, that something they are about to do is wrong and to stop. I tell my students, **if it feels wrong, it usually is wrong**. Teaching our children to ignore their gut reactions will weaken their intuition. We must guide them to mindfully become aware of their instincts and to rely on them, counteracting that weakness by strengthening their skills.

Before we can teach our children to trust their instincts, we need to teach them to recognize their instincts and differentiate between the discomfort that comes from an unfamiliar situation and the discomfort that comes from considering an immoral action. We can teach them to stop and think, **How do I feel about this situation? Why do I feel that way? Is my moral compass trying to tell me something?**

Let's say a situation makes a child uncomfortable. First they need to ask, **Why do I feel uncomfortable?** Perhaps they are trying out for the school orchestra, but are scared of the performance. Getting up onstage in front of people feels uncomfortable and scary because it is new, but it is not wrong. This is the kind of discomfort worth pushing through. A mindful response might be to take a deep breath, look around, and remind themselves that everyone gets nervous before performances—even seasoned performers—and that even if they make a mistake, everyone does, and the world will not end with this one. Although they are afraid, they will be safe, and they can proceed despite their discomfort. This is not the uncomfortable feeling that has to do with morality.

Another child might be uncomfortable because their group of friends is passing around a list of classmates they have designated as "Losers." The child asks, **Why do I feel uncomfortable?** She realizes that, while she does not like any of the classmates on the list, she knows that she would be deeply hurt to be on the list, and she would not want to hurt someone else in the same way. Her discomfort comes from knowing that her classmates are doing something harmful and from knowing she would feel shame if her parents, or other people she respects, were to find out.

Discomfort can mean many things, and addressing it mindfully means stopping when we feel it, asking why we are feeling it, and responding appropriately to the situation. When it comes to how we treat others, it is safe to say, **if it feels wrong, it is wrong**.

Most of us have had a failure of empathy at some point in our lives. Many of us have said something thoughtless, hurt someone's feelings, or even done real damage to a relationship, whether unintentionally or because we acted out in a moment of anger. Like us, our children will make mistakes. At some point, even the shyest, least popular child will most likely do something to hurt someone else. We can teach them to try and prevent that, but just as importantly, we have to teach them to be accountable for their actions, to take responsibility, and to sincerely apologize.

Sometimes, the public and permanent nature of the Internet can be turned to moral advantage. Like politicians who have offended, a child who has publicly humiliated or insulted a classmate can make their apology as public as the original offense. This is not meant simply to shame or humiliate the offender but to give them a platform with which to admit they were wrong and try to redress the balance of their actions. Empathy means not only recognizing when we have done something wrong or harmful but also seeking to redress or repair that harm.

Recognizing Our Impact

BEING MINDFUL AS parents means being aware of the impact our own actions have on our children. We set examples for them, and we set expectations. Many of us may have had those moments when, in the middle of a sentence, we stop and realize *I am turning into my mother!* Whether we greet that realization with pleasure or horror may depend on our relationship to our own mother. Some of us hope to emulate our parents, while others define our lives by striving not to be like them. Regardless, our choices, actions, and beliefs are framed by an awareness of how those most important adults in our lives conducted themselves.

Though many of our children will probably rebel and complain about us no matter what we do, they will model their behaviors, beliefs, and values on ours, and it is important to stop and think, throughout our lives, **Is this what I want my child to learn?**

As a teacher, I have found that my job was not only to teach curriculum but to carefully choose my words and my reactions in order to do my job to the best of my ability. The way children feel about themselves has a direct impact on their success, both educationally and emotionally. The unfortunate reality is that our children learn the most by watching and modeling themselves on us. Unfortunately, this is not so easy as a parent, because parenting is not a job and children are not products. As a teacher I am focused on my job in the moment. I am teaching while I am working, and when that performance is done for the day, I am done. When I am parenting, I am not performing, and I am not only a parent. I am also being myself. I am a parent, but I am also a spouse, a sister, a friend, a neighbor, and a person. Mindfully modeling behaviors for our children does not mean being perfect! In modeling mindful use of technology, I have learned as I went along. Sometimes I spent too much or too little time doing one thing or another. This is new for us, as well as for our children! Making errors and miscalculations along the way just means that it is time to try something new.

As parents, and as educators, we have all seen that children model both our good and bad behavior. I do not think it is a stifling feeling. Unfortunately for me, my children have picked up as many of my bad habits as they have of the good. Being mindful in our lives means more than paying attention to the moment we are in; it means considering the impact we will have on the world around us, which is almost always greater than we realize. But this does not mean being perfect so that our children will be perfect. It just means paying attention to what we are doing and why, as much for ourselves as for them.

We must teach this awareness to our children. We can teach them empathy, and to understand how others feel, but we can teach them, too, to think carefully about who they want to emulate and to consider who may be emulating them. Some children are leaders, and some are followers. Most are a little bit of both. A girl who is a natural leader may not realize how closely her peers follow and imitate the things she does and says; she needs to come to understand that her actions have a large impact on those around her and that empathy and good judgment are therefore all the more important. A boy who prefers to take his social cues from his friends needs to realize that just because he is not taking the lead does not mean that he has any less responsibility to act with empathy and good intent. His actions, kind or unkind, carry as much weight as anyone else's.

It is easy for children to feel powerless in their environments. Teachers, coaches, and parents all restrict children's action in some way, and it is common for them to feel as though their actions do not matter. We must teach them that, large or small, every choice they make has an impact on their surroundings. The importance of educating our children to use technology with this in mind will create a more civil cyber community than the one so many of our children are now taking part in. We need to show them that technology should be used with good intent and not as a weapon. Creating a civil society means teaching our children to make good decisions, but without making them feel that they have to be flawless. We need to send the message that mistakes are rarely catastrophic, and that it is never too late to change and grow at any age.

Creating Mindful Habits

PART OF FORMING healthy technology habits means examining what is working for us and what is not. The definition of a habit is an action we do by default, without thinking, and some of the habits we fall into are negative ones. Many of us have struggled to quit biting our nails, to change our diets, to add an exercise routine, or to get more sleep. Sometimes this is because the bad habit is fun or relieves stress. People smoke because it keeps them calm, not because they want to get cancer, and people overindulge in sweets because they taste good, not because they want high blood sugar. People who go to bed too late want to feel good about accomplishing just one more thing or want to cram in some free time before getting up and doing it all over again; they aren't strategically setting themselves up to be tired and grouchy in the morning. When we address our negative habits, it is important to acknowledge that we have them because they serve a need for us. Though they are ultimately damaging, we get some sort of immediate benefit from them. When our children engage in destructive online habits, it is important to remember that they are doing it for a reason, and we can help them to find better ways to meet those needs.

In the sections that follow, you will find the handout worksheets that I give out at my student presentations. This is a good solid place to start the much-needed conversation with your child or student. It may be easier to download them from the Don't Press Send Campaign website at www.DontPressSend.org under "Education" and "Documents for Download." Keeping these in a visible place in your home will help remind you and reinforce the use of a more mindful approach to technology. Talking with our children about which habits are healthy and which are not is a good first step toward using technology in a more positive manner.

When we think about changing our children's technology habits, the first step is to begin being mindful, recognizing that every action we take is a choice. Every time someone who is trying to watch their weight is tempted by the cookies or snacks screaming their name while shopping, they are making a choice to continue a bad habit and not to push the cart through to the next aisle, removing the temptation. We can talk to our children about their technology habits and identify what they are doing over and over, what is working for them, and what is working against them. Taking a lighthearted approach is best. As we know, when we say "don't," they will.

For example, fourteen-year-old Tara might have a habit of checking social media right after dinner, before she starts her homework. Each night she goes to her favorite social media site, planning just to check in for a few minutes and maybe chat briefly with a friend before going on to her homework. Yet every night, Tara finds that those few minutes drag on into hours as she checks all her friends' accounts, chats, and comments on multiple posts. By the time she starts her homework, she is already tired and possibly in a negative place because of a post she may have read. She keeps her phone by her side while she works and is constantly interrupted and distracted by texts. Combined, all of those things—negative mood, distraction, interruption, and multitasking—do not make for a great study environment.

One response to the situation might be to tell Tara, "Stop spending so much time on social media!" There is no reason she has to check her phone each time she gets a text, so she should stop doing that. This seems logical: her problem is that she gets distracted, minutes turn into hours, and if she simply disciplined herself better, she would not have a problem. However, this is not helpful. If she had the willpower to curb her social media use like that, she would already be using it.

Instead, we need to work with our children to create an environment where they will be successful. We need to help them identify the obstacles in their paths and help them develop ways to make it easy to succeed. Helping Tara does not mean barring her from her technology, and it does not mean leaving her alone and telling her to just do better. Tara's mother might realize that Tara's problem begins right after dinner, when she checks her social media accounts before starting her homework. Standard behavior modifications are always great—setting goals and offering rewards. We might tell our children that if they succeed in shutting down their phone on time all week, they will get something they have been wanting. Motivation works. Just like no one goes to work for free, no one takes the difficult path of changing their behavior without a concrete reason.

Tara and her mother might work together to come up with a plan where Tara checks social media *before* dinner, so that there is a natural breaking point when she is called to the table. Additionally, Tara gets distracted by her phone while doing her homework. If Tara and her parents declare her homework area a phone-free zone while she is working, the distraction is gone, and she does not need superhuman willpower to stay focused on her work.

Too often, we frame bad habits as the result of our own moral failings or lack of good character, when often they are formed when we act mindlessly, reacting to the things that happen around us without ever stopping, stepping back, and asking, *Why am I doing things this way?* For ourselves and for our children, we need to begin taking that step back from our routines and habits and looking at the places where we reinforce our own bad habits. We can begin to identify ways to set ourselves up for success and create new, positive habits to replace our old bad ones.

The good news is that once we have formed new habits, those will become our new default behaviors. Breaking bad habits is far, far easier when they are being replaced with new, good habits that make us feel better about our own lives. If we can take the time to sit down with our children and talk to them about the impact technology has on their lives, both negative and positive, we can help them to identify the things they need to change. Using the guidelines and techniques in this book, you can help your child to become mindful about their behavior, online and off. When they make a habit of stopping and pausing before they post, it will become automatic.

Hindsight is twenty-twenty. If I knew when I first gave my children cell phones all the things I know now, I would have gone about things differently. For one, I would not have been so quick to give my children technology they were ill-prepared for at such a young age. In this book, I have focused on providing tips and guidelines for parents whose children are already using personal technology on a regular basis, but I also want to reach those parents who have not yet given their children cell phones—to give them a chance to pause and think before they take that step.

This book is an attempt not only to be honest about our struggles as parents of tech-savvy kids, but to help the parent to create a healthy place for technology from the start. My hope is that these techniques can be used as part of an early-intervention strategy, in addition to helping those of us already in the thick of it, trying to break the bad habits our children have formed. I hope to help others prevent the patterns I see in my own children. My seventeen-year-old's phone is unfortunately an appendage that I cannot pry away from him, but my thirteen-year-old twins are in a better position because I learned from my experiences with him.

The Don't Press Send Campaign began as I sat at the sixth grade parents' orientation and listened to my children's principal talk about all of the problems they had been having with students' use of technology. Afterward, I asked her if she would back me up if I came up with a program to address these issues. After about two months, I gave my presentation to the sixth graders. The principal was very pleased with the outcome and asked me to return to present to the seventh and eighth grade. From that point on, the program began to flourish by word of mouth, and I was asked to speak at numerous schools. It is because of the Don't Press Send Campaign that my twins are doing better with their use of technology. I have learned so much, and I have had to enforce within my own family what I am trying to strengthen in everyone else's.

An ounce of prevention is worth a pound of cure. I wish I had this book available to me before my children entered this all-consuming world of technology. I always say, "Pick your hard," because both are difficult: setting rules from the beginning, and detoxing children who are already immersed in social media. I believe that it is easier to set ground rules from the beginning than to try and backpedal once children have already developed their habits and patterns. If you teach children from the start to eat healthy, they will continue to eat well. If you started them off on junk food, forcing them to switch to broccoli would be hard. Those of us in the middle of this need to do damage control, but those who have not yet started down the path have the power to prevent.

As I close this book, I hope that it has lessened your anxiety regarding technology use and empowered you to provide your children with some good, sound guidelines. Though it may feel like a new frontier in parenting, this is simply another conversation that we need to have, just as we do with other potentially dangerous subjects. I always like to think of the acronym KISS—Keep It Simple, Stupid! And so I have tried to make all of the suggestions from this book easy to access. In the vein of KISS, downloading my Don't Press Send app is a quick, easy, and simple way to ensure that your children learn strategies and create boundaries. Each pledge is a conversation in itself. You can always reread this book and the worksheets at the back, which can also be downloaded online at DontPressSend.org—review them with your children from time to time, or put them on the refrigerator, next to the family computer, or in your child's bedroom.

If there is one more thing I would hope you take away from this book, it is this—kids will be kids, and part of being a kid and growing up is making mistakes. Let's teach them not to document theirs! If they do not test the boundaries as children or teenagers, they will do it as young adults, when the consequences of their errors can be far, far greater. Let us teach them to push the limits in ways that are safe, and to keep their mistakes private and off the Internet.

Best of luck with your technological parenting journey! It is my hope that this book is of service to you and your family.

Each of the following pages can be digitally downloaded off
www.DontPressSend.org under the Education tab.

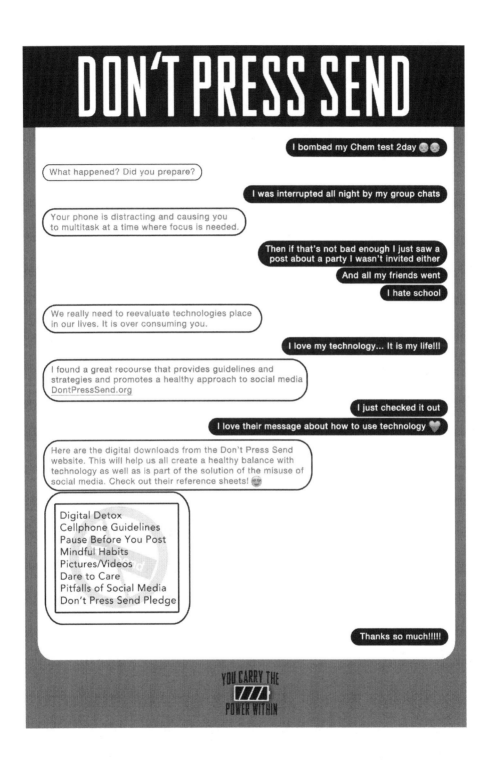

REFERENCE SHEETS

DIGITAL DETOX

Just as we examine our dietary health habits, we must also examine our social and emotional health habits. Taking a closer look at our relationship with technology will help us to create healthier patterns of behavior. Many of us have detoxed to help cleanse our physical body. Similarly, digitally detoxing may cleanse our psychological health by evaluating technology's place in our lives.

I challenge your family to take the Digital Detox and encourage you to evaluate your personal relationship with technology. I hope the result will serve as a guide for you to implement a more mindful lifestyle.

ılı, DIGITAL DETOX

MINDFUL MONDAY

Look up! Pay attention on purpose. Be present in each and every task you do.
» Make eye contact
» Smile at passing strangers
» Notice the beauty around you

TECH-FREE TUESDAY

Necessary use only! (i.e., work or school assignments). Avoid:
» Cell phone use
» Video games
» Checking emails
» Social media

WEB-WITHDRAWAL WEDNESDAY

Avoid the temptation!
» No online shopping
» No Facebook browsing
» No surfing the net

THOUGHTFUL THURSDAY

Careful, kind communication! Use social media in a positive manner.
» Send an inspirational quote
» Share an uplifting story
» Send a funny video
» Compliment a friend via social media
****No self promotion

FREEDOM FRIDAY

Kick off your weekend, free of digital distraction
» Go to an event and enjoy it for what it is without posting or boasting

SOCIAL SATURDAY

Take the media out of social!
» Be fully present in whatever you do
» Actively participate in conversation
» Be a good listener
» Be aware of body language

SIMPLE SUNDAY

Go "Old School"!
» Play a simple card game
» Play a board game
» Reflect on technology's place in your life
» Use it for all the good it has to offer
» Implement a healthy balance with technology

ⅰ⃰ CELL PHONE GUIDELINES

» **Set a reasonable time for all technology to be docked in a central location for the evening (e.g., the kitchen).**

» **Do not allow cell phones to be used as alarm clocks.**
This prevents participation in unkind dialogue (nasty grams), which usually occurs during the night hours. It also helps prevent the need to be overly connected.

» **Homework hours are cell phone-free hours.**
This avoids distraction and over-connection.

» **No technology at the table at home or at a restaurant.**
This encourages conversation and improves social skills.

» **No technology on short car rides.**
This is invaluable time where good conversations can be had. The 15-30 minute car ride provides an undisturbed arena that is precious and rare. Don't waste it.

||. PAUSE BEFORE YOU POST

ASK YOURSELF THESE QUESTIONS BEFORE YOU PRESS SEND:

- » Would I say what I typed face to face? (Kindness)
- » Did I ask permission to send this photo or video? (Respect)
- » Am I being mindful of others with my post? (Mindfulness)
- » Would this make me feel good if I received it? (Empathy)
- » Is my text's intent clear without misunderstanding? (Perception)
- » Is this post a reflection of the true person I am? (Self-Respect)
- » Is this personal or private? Does it need to be shared? (Privacy)
- » Am I spreading negativity? (Intent)

⑈, MINDFUL HABITS

Encourage/Model Mindful Behavior

» **Pay attention on purpose.**
Learn to be fully present wherever and whatever you are doing. Pleasant or unpleasant, learn to just be. Take notice of the beauty all around you.

» **Be present at all events.**
Be an active participant and do not allow your focus to be about caputuring the perfect photo or overly documenting the event.

» **Do one thing at a time.**
Give your full attention to the task at hand or to the people with whom you are present. Learning to concentrate and giving your full attention to one task at a time will foster a mindful attitude.

» **Learn to take a mindful pause before you post.**
Recognize the difference between a reaction and a response. Take a mindful breath and think about how— and if—you should respond.

» **Be respectful of others' space.**
Use your technology in areas where it will not be intrusive. Refrain from talking on your phone in the presence of others.

ⅲ. PICTURE/VIDEO GUIDELINES

DO NOT:	DO:
Send photos/video that may make someone feel excluded	Take pictures to capture a moment or memory and share with those who are in the photo
Take and/or post pictures, videos, or voice recordings without permission	Ask these questions: » "Can I take your photo, video, or voice recording?" » "Can I post/share this picture, video or voice recording?"
Send photos/video of you or anyone else without clothing on	Send pictures that promote a good self image of respect of yourself and others

Iıı DARE TO CARE

Consider the following examples, and encourage your children to use social media with good intent.

» Compliment a classmate.

» Send an appropriate and funny joke or video.

» Share an inspirational story or quote.

» Send an apology if you have hurt someone.

» Take a funny picture of yourself.

» Unplug for an hour or two and write down how you feel.

» Write a list of the positives and negatives of technology and incorporate the positives.

» Post something without checking for the number of "likes."

» Go through your friends and followers list and delete those who are not your "true" friends, remembering that not everyone should have access to you.
(Protect Your Privacy)

lll, PITFALLS OF SOCIAL MEDIA

PITFALL	RESULT
The barrier of the screen	Emotional disconnection
Friends and followers	False sense of friendship
Overattachment to devices	Addiction
Multitasking	Antimindful behavior
Oversharing	Voyeuristic behavior
Excessive posting	Narcissistic behavior
Browsing through others' profiles	Destructive, nonproductive use of time
Anonymous sites	No accountability
The "like" button	Overly valuing peers' feedback
TWI/TWE (texting while intoxicated/ emotional)	Regret

—

ⅼⅼⅼ DON'T PRESS SEND PLEDGE ®

- » I will carefully choose who I allow to have my cell phone number.
- » I will not give anyone account information such as passwords or answers to security questions.
- » I will choose followers/friends with the understanding that not everyone is my "true" friend.
- » I will not type or send messages that I would not say face-to-face.
- » I am aware that "the screen" creates an emotional disconnect, and I will choose to use Kind and Careful communication.
- » When reading any text or post, I will remember to mindfully respond and not impulsively react.
- » I am aware of the dangers that anonymous sites and apps present and will choose not to partake.
- » I will ask permission before taking and/or posting photos or recordings of anyone, valuing my privacy and respecting the privacy of others.
- » I will not send any pictures or videos of myself or anyone else without clothing on.
- » If something is making me feel uncomfortable or unhappy, I will make the choice to unfriend, unfollow, delete, block, turn off, or step away from my device.
- » I will keep open communication with a trusted adult regarding online interactions.
- » I will not post group pictures of an event, knowing that exclusion is very hurtful.
- » I am aware of the dangerous habit of posting things in order to get a number of "Likes."
- » I will not have my cell phone accessible during homework hours and will set a reasonable time for it to be docked for the evening.
- » I will choose to use an alarm clock, and not a cell phone because I know it creates an unhealthy attachment and will prevent me from engaging in potentially harmful dialogue.
- » I am aware of the ramifications of my actions if I send something that is inappropriate or hurtful to another and how it could affect my future.
- » I promise not to send any pictures or texts that do not show respect to others or myself.
- » I will try my best to use Kind and Careful communication while using all technology and share my knowledge with my peers to aid in the "DON'T PRESS SEND" Campaign.

_____   _____
STUDENT SIGNATURE   PARENT/GUARDIAN SIGNATURE

WE CARRY THE POWER WITHIN

Made in the USA
Middletown, DE
27 July 2017